Breaking Through
to Your Highest Potential

Understanding Self-Esteem
and Making It Work for You

by
Jimmy Reader

Tulsa, Oklahoma

Breaking Through to Your Highest Potential
Understanding Self-Esteem and Making It Work for You
ISBN 0-89274-490-1
Copyright © 1988 by Jimmy Reader
412 S. F
Wellington, Kansas 67152

Published by Honor Books
P. O. Box 35035
Tulsa, Oklahoma 74153

Contents

Part III: Develop an Understanding

Part IV: Make It Work

Part V: The Last Word

Foreword

When I first read Jimmy Reader's critique of my book on Self-Esteem (in section 2 of this book), I was impressed. Here was a young pastor and seminary student who was asking the right questions. And he was "right on" with honest and fair answers. We need much more of that in the Church. This book can help you with both the questions and the answers.

A good deal of work needs to be done by Christians to develop an approach to the Christian faith that will glorify God by honoring human beings. We need to be biblically sound, but we also need to make use of the best insights from psychology and the human potential movement of today. Jimmy's "potentiality thinking" is a good step in that direction.

He has done an excellent job in this book of bringing together two tremendously important subjects: Self-Esteem and Leadership. I consider Leadership to be a central responsibility of the human person by virtue of creation and redemption. In our approach to leadership, the dignity of the individual is paramount, and our responsibility for ourselves and others should be pre-eminent. This book develops these things in an inspiring, straight-forward manner.

Soon after I met Jimmy, I told him, "You're Terrific!" I'm excited about the way he has applied those words to a basic attitude that can help us all to build self-esteem in tomorrow's leaders.

Robert H. Schuller

Preface

When I started writing this book, it was supposed to be about leadership training. The question I wanted to answer was: "How can we develop good, long-term leadership for our churches?" The answer, I thought, lay in the area of preparing people to be servants. I was convinced that if we adopted the attitude of servants toward God, toward others in the Church, and toward the world, we would produce leaders who could provide sound, responsible direction for the Church.

As I began my research, I quickly realized that many pastors and lay leaders had already adopted the servant attitude. They believed they were called to serve God and the people. But it seemed to me that we were still not providing the effective leadership our churches needed. I was sure there had to be something more.

The answer came as a new insight to me: *we must build self-esteem in the people who attend our churches.* I know pastors and other church leaders who are sincere and faithful servants of the Church and of God, but who are weak and ineffective as leaders. They provide little guidance for their churches and make no impact at all on the world outside the Church. What they lack is self-confidence, enthusiasm for their dreams and goals, and determination to lead the Church of Jesus Christ forward into new and greater challenges. In my opinion, these people lack these attributes because they lack self-esteem.

We need to prepare people who will be leaders both in the Church and in the world. They need to be persons who are mature and responsible, ready to take the initiative in decision-making among their peers. They need to make decisions that will benefit the greatest number of people possible. That kind of decisive leadership requires people with healthy self-esteem.

When I got to this point in my thinking, I remembered a book which I had put away on my library shelf a couple of years earlier. It is called *Self-Esteem: The New Reformation* by Dr. Robert H. Schuller. In that book, I found what I needed to set me thinking in the direction I knew I must go. So I decided to write a critique of that book as a part of this one. When I sent a copy of the critique to Dr. Schuller, asking for his comments, he wrote back a very encouraging letter with this closing comment: "You're Terrific!"

In those two words, I found the simple, positive attitude which is the key to building up self-esteem in others: *tell them they're terrific*. Let people know how important, how beautiful, they are. Remind them of all the good things they are doing. Make them feel good about themselves. What better way to prepare people who will become the leaders of tomorrow's world than by building up their self-esteem?

Don't dismiss this concept too quickly as a simplistic, secular or humanistic approach to this subject. As you read this book, you will discover that self-esteem (like leadership) is at the core of the Gospel. The twin concepts of Creation and New Creation, as they are presented in the Old and New Testaments of the Bible, reveal the fundamental importance of human beings to God and to the divine mission of reconciling the world to Him. So stay with me, keep an open mind, and read carefully. My thinking was changed in the process of researching and writing this book. Perhaps yours will be transformed also, as you read it.

You may not be a theologian or a minister. You may not know much about the Bible. You may not even be a Christian. That's all right. You can read this book, too. It will help you. It will change your attitude toward yourself, and thereby change your attitude toward others. It will help you learn effective ways to build self-esteem in others, and thereby build up your own sense of self-worth. And it will help you learn how to prepare other persons (perhaps your children) to become leaders in tomorrow's world.

Jimmy Reader

Acknowledgments and Dedication

I want to thank Dr. Robert H. Schuller for all his help. He encouraged me in the writing of this book through several letters, books and tapes he sent me. He invited me to a private retreat for theological discussion on the issue of self-esteem and leadership. His books have been invaluable in helping me change my thinking and my attitude toward others. My experience in putting these ideas to the test is reflected in these pages.

I want to thank Dr. Richard S. Armstrong, my senior adviser at Princeton Theological Seminary. This book originally developed as a thesis for my Master of Divinity degree at the seminary. Dr. Armstrong gave me permission to develop my thesis in the form of a book for the popular market. I have used some of his suggestions, especially in the footnotes, to correct my views on some issues. Some of what I had first written seemed to be out-of-touch with the realities of life for persons caught in economic and politically oppressive situations. I hope I have corrected that oversight, or at least presented a more balanced view.

I also want to thank the First Baptist Church of Wellington, Kansas. The members of that church helped me work through many of these ideas in the form of sermons and evening seminars. They listened responsively, encouraged me generously, and suggested some of the ideas contained in the book (or, at least, helped to refine some of my own ideas in discussions). They allowed me a little extra time in the first months of my pastoral ministry there so I could finish the writing of the book.

My wife, Ginny, worked hard throughout this project to build up my self-esteem, encouraging and supporting me. She helped me (probably more than I realize) to work out many of these ideas.

Some of what is in this book comes out of our experience together as parents in the rearing of our four children: Sheri, Bob, Philip, and Michelle. I want to thank them, too, for the inspiration they have been in learning from us about maturity, responsibility, initiative, and self-esteem (all key ingredients of leadership). They have been the inspiration for my approach to this subject. I have thought a great deal about the world as it will be in the year 2020 A.D., when our children will be at the prime of their lives. What kind of leaders will the world need then? And what kind of leadership will our children provide as adults? So I thank them for their help, unknown though it was to them.

Finally, I want to dedicate this book to the leaders of tomorrow's world. All of them. I hope that our churches will learn in this generation more effective ways to prepare people to become leaders of succeeding generations. I hope our young people, especially, will be taught and inspired by our adults today to become mature, responsible persons who will take the initiative among their peers to make decisions that will benefit the greatest number of people possible. That's leadership. And that's what this book is about.

Part I:
Catch the Vision

1

What's in a Name

Portrait of a Leader[1]

He was born in an obscure village, the child of a peasant woman. He grew up in still another village, where he worked in a carpenter shop until he was thirty. Then for three years he was an itinerant preacher.

He never wrote a book. He never held an office. He never had a family or owned a house. He didn't go to college.

He never traveled 200 miles from the place where he was born. He did none of the things one usually associates with greatness.

He had no credentials but himself.

He was only 33 when public opinion turned against him. His friends ran away. He was turned over to his enemies and went through the mockery of a trial. He was nailed to a cross between two thieves. When he was dying, his executioners gambled for his clothing, the only property he had on earth. When he was dead, he was laid in a borrowed grave through the pity of a friend.

Does this narrative sound like the portrait of a leader? Does it describe for you the life of someone you would

---

[1]Usually entitled "One Solitary Life"; author unknown.

17

consider to be the greatest leader of human beings who ever lived? Yet such a leader is exactly what these anonymously written words describe.

Here is the rest of the quotation:

> Nineteen centuries have come and gone, and today he is the central figure of the human race, the leader of mankind's progress.

> All the armies that ever marched, all the navies that ever sailed, all the parliaments that ever sat, all the kings that ever reigned, put together, have not affected the life of man on earth as much as that One Solitary Life.

These words describe, of course, the life of a man called Jesus of Nazareth. The Christian Church gave Him the title of Christ, the Anointed One. Jesus Christ, through the force of His personality and the power of His love, has transformed our world over the centuries which have intervened between Him and us. As the Church has passed on His teachings, as men and women have put their faith in Him, as we have lived our lives according to His example, teachings and spiritual presence, our world has been slowly changed.

What was there about Jesus – which He has passed on to each new generation of believers – that has such a transforming power? What did He teach? What example did He give us? What is this force, in His Spirit made available to us, that has enabled the Church to become a life-changing presence in the world? What potential change does the future hold for those who are ready to live according to the teaching, example, and presence of Jesus Christ?

The answer to these questions is what this book is all about. But before we can examine these answers, we must define leadership in more detail:

If we think of leaders only as those few persons at the top who tell everyone else what to do, we will miss the point of this whole discussion. We must stop thinking of leadership in terms of "chiefs and Indians," of officers and enlisted men, of CEOs and subordinates. Instead we must begin to see everyone we meet as a leader regardless of position. We must begin to envision a new system and order in which each individual has a share in the decision-making process.

As Robert Schuller suggests in his lectures at his Institutes of Successful Church Leadership,[2] the first in each of these sets of choices – "chiefs," officers, CEOs – gives us a false impression of what real leadership is. A leader is not one who exercises power and authority over others, but one who sets the example for them to follow.

Leaders are mature, responsible persons who take the initiative in decision-making among their peers.

This definition of leadership applies to persons of all ages, at all levels of maturity.

A six-year-old boy can be mature and responsible, on the level of his peers, and can learn to take the initiative in whatever decisions he and his friends make about appropriate behavior for them. That's leadership.

A 16-year-old girl can be mature and responsible, in relation to her peers, and can take the initiative in making

---

[2]We will consider Schuller's ideas more carefully in Part II.

decisions about her behavior with her boyfriend or with her friends at a party or among her classmates at school.

A 32-year-old business executive should certainly have reached a level of maturity and responsibility that will enable him or her to make good choices in taking the initiative on the job, at home, and among friends and associates.

Take any example you want – a person at any age, in any circumstance – and this definition will hold up. Follow it through to the highest levels of decision-making and leadership as we have traditionally perceived it, and it is still true: a leader is one who takes the initiative in decision-making.

As I was writing this book, in the fall of 1985, Mikhail Gorbachev and Ronald Reagan were holding a summit meeting in Geneva, Switzerland. Now in 1988, as I am preparing the manuscript for final publication, these two, the leaders of the most powerful nations on earth, have just concluded a second summit meeting in Moscow.

These men hold the fate of the world in their hands. The decisions they make, if any are made at all, will affect the future course of history. Their peers are the leaders of the nations of the world. They need to take the initiative in deciding to curtail the development and deployment of nuclear arms and, perhaps, of weapons in space. They must be mature and responsible as – with their peers looking on – they take the initiative in providing the dynamic leadership our world so desperately needs at this moment.

Leaders are persons whose healthy self-esteem frees them to make responsible choices that will lead to a better life for other people.

This secondary definition applies to Gorbachev and Reagan – and to their successors. Are our leaders going to be bound by their fears and mistrust of each other and the nations they represent? Will they refuse to make choices that will lead to a better life for all people? Or will they have the courage to be the leaders that our world needs today? Will they make the responsible choices that will make possible a better life for us and our posterity? (Some would say that without arms control, there will be no hope of life at all for future generations.)

A healthy self-esteem is vital to good leadership. Self-esteem, as we will see in the rest of this book, enables us to trust others because we trust ourselves. It enables us to live with courage and hope. It opens the potential for living with gentleness and patience and peace. It is linked together with faith, with positive possibility-thinking – or what I call Potentiality Thinking.[3] Self-esteem gives any person strength and inner power and full confidence. It is the key to successful leadership, as I am defining it here.

That's important – don't miss it. I am offering a new definition of *leadership*. The traditional concept of leaders is too limited for the world as it is becoming. We are living in an age of transition. We cannot return to the past. We cannot be limited to past concepts, ideas and definitions. We must open ourselves to the future without knowing for sure quite what that future holds.

In the last decade, a whole new career has opened. up. We now have persons who are called "futurists." By education, job title and commitment, they are prepared to help us understand what the future may be like before it

---

[3] See Chapter 1, Part III.

comes so we can be more fully prepared for it. We are not talking about horoscopes, astrology or spiritist prognosticators. We are referring to sound sociological research in which present trends and past experiences are examined and considered in an attempt to help us formulate new ways of thinking and acting that will prepare us to live in the world of the future.

That is what we in the Church need to do. We need to prepare leaders for tomorrow's world. In order to do that, first of all, we need to believe that there will be a world in the next century to prepare for. We need to learn to live in hope.

Some people are convinced that the end of the world, as prophesied in the Bible, will come before the turn of the next century, before the year 2000. Perhaps it will. I am certainly not in any position to declare absolutely that it will not. But what if the world doesn't end? What if we are still here to see the year 2001? What if churches are still struggling, and people are still going to work, getting married, having families and trying to stay alive? What then?

The world of the 21st century, if there is one (and I believe there will be), will need new leaders. It *will need persons who are mature and responsible, persons who will take the initiative among their peers to make decisions that will lead to a better life for all people.* And that is the business of the Church.

Jesus came to change the world – to bring light into the darkness, to bring love in place of hatred, to bring the Kingdom of God on earth. When Jesus ascended into heaven, He left behind the Church – a group of believers in every generation whose task and calling it is to be about the work of changing the world. As followers of Christ, we believe that we know the truth, that we have "good news of great joy for all people," news that will transform their lives, news that will bring them into a new life. If that is so, then we ought to get on with our work of preparing people in the Church to be leaders in the world.

You may be familiar with the words of Shakespeare:

What's in a name? That which we call a rose
By any other name would smell as sweet.[4]

That may be true of roses, but it doesn't apply here. It does matter what we think the word *leader* means. How we define and understand this word makes all the difference in whether we expect to be leaders ourselves and in how we train our young people to become leaders in tomorrow's world.

As we work at preparing ourselves and others for leadership, there are two other words we need to keep in mind: *integrity* and *self-esteem*. Like the word *leader*, each of these words is full of meaning. We could fill up whole books trying to describe these attributes and what people are like who possess them. In fact, even though we will not use these words constantly throughout the remainder of this book, they represent the foundational concepts behind all that we will say about leadership.

---

[4]Bartlett, John. *Familiar Quotations: A Collection* of Passages, Phrases, and Proverbs Traced to Their Sources in Ancient and Modern Literature. 11th Edition. (Boston: Little, Brown and Company, 1938), p. 78. From William Shakespeare's *Romeo and Juliet*, Act II, Scene 2, Line 43.

So before we press on, I would like to examine the meanings of these vital words. To do that, I want to give you another word for each of the letters which compose them. Even then, the combination of ideas behind all of these words will only begin to scratch the surface of the deep, rich, full meaning of *leadership*.

Integrity

Individual

A person with integrity is an individual, one who stands apart from others, one who can be easily distinguished from all other people. A person who is an individual is different. That's why we have so few true individuals and so few real leaders. Few of us want to be different. We try so hard to be like everyone else and not to stand out.

Leaders are persons who know they are special and unique. They believe that God created each of us to be an "original." Each person on earth has something unique to offer this world. So we need to cultivate our uniqueness, to let it flower and bloom. We must dare to be different, in the sense that we are willing to be seen for who and what we are. We must learn to say to the world: "Here I am; and here's what I have to give you."

True individuals refuse to be pulled along by others into their way of thinking. They think for themselves. Contrary to their peers, they decide that, if necessary, they will do what is best for themselves and for the world, regardless of the opinions of others. They have the courage to follow a lifestyle that will benefit the greatest number of people. And they boldly set an example for others to learn from.

Natural

Every word has connotations for some people which are not shared by others because of different life experiences. The word *natural* has acquired many strange meanings in recent years. But as I am defining it here, to be natural is to be plain and unsophisticated, making no pretense of being something we are not. If that is what natural is, then much of the world (especially in America and Europe) is working very hard to be unnatural.

If we strip away all the makeup and fancy jewelry, if we dress in simple clothing, we are being natural – outwardly. In the same way, inwardly, if we strip away all the pretenses of being different from what we really are, we are being natural. Too many people are living as if they are at a costume party all the time, trying to make other people guess who they really are.

Leaders, as we are defining the term in this book, will choose to live naturally. They will be spontaneous, with innate and ingrained characteristics that are not spoiled by trying to be something they are not. They will choose not to be sophisticated, but instead to lead simple, unadorned lives emotionally and spiritually (and, perhaps, physically). They will risk the danger of other people seeing them as they really are because they are persons filled with love, joy, peace, and wisdom. They will have the inner strength to be themselves. And that inner strength will give them the authority they will need as leaders in this world.

Trustworthy

We can risk being natural when we are naturally trustworthy. When we follow our instincts and do what we know is right, we can be trusted to do what is best for others, as well as for ourselves. And that makes us trustworthy.[5]

Leaders can be trusted not to change under pressure. A notable example is Daniel, whose story is found in the Bible book by that name. His enemies knew that he prayed to God three times a day. When they wanted to get rid of him, they influenced the king to issue a decree that no one could pray to any god or man for the following 30 days at the risk of death. Daniel did not fail his enemies; he proved trustworthy even to them. He refused to change under pressure, and continued to pray each day at his appointed times. (If the story is not familiar to you, you may be interested to know that Daniel was miraculously protected and delivered, ending up in a stronger position than ever.)

Leaders can be described with any of these other synonyms: reliable, true, sincere, honest, honorable, loyal, faithful, dependable, steady and conscientious. Leaders are persons who can be trusted; and persons who can be trusted naturally step into positions of leadership wherever they go.

Energetic

Persons with integrity find the physical, moral and spiritual energy necessary to sustain them through long years of testing and triumph. They are energetic, in the richest sense of that word. They are not superficially enthusiastic – like fair-weather fans at a football game.

---

[5]You may be thinking that human beings are sinners and cannot be trusted to follow their natural instincts. But stay with me until we talk about the transformation of the New Creation. That makes all the difference.

They persevere under all circumstances, and follow through with commitments to other people. They do not give up in the face of failure. Neither do they give up when they first experience success, thinking that now they can rest. Through testing and triumph, leaders keep on with their commitment to bring about a better life for as many people as possible.

Energetic persons are industrious and aggressive in everything they do. They have the stamina and determination to see each job, commitment and relationship through to its successful conclusion. They are dynamic, vigorous and active in their attitudes and in the way they do their work. They are able to sustain their drive toward a goal by renewing their energy through expending it in the accomplishment of that goal. They know they will have the energy (physical, emotional and spiritual) they will need tomorrow only if they expend what they have today in the best possible way.

Growing

Leaders never stop learning. They continue to grow and mature as human beings. They learn from the experiences, advice and circumstances of others. They learn from their own experiences of both failure and success. They keep their eyes open and their minds free to learn all they can about how to become better persons.

Persons with integrity continue to mature; they are never content with what they have learned or attained up to that point. They expand, stretch, develop and extend themselves beyond where they are at the moment. They are always open to the future with hope and confidence for a better day for all people. They intend to be a part of that better day.

Responsible

Leaders know they are accountable. They are aware that no one is totally free to do as they please. None of us can go our own way – completely independent, stubborn and rebellious. We are all accountable to others for what we do and how we live. Children are accountable to their parents. Parents are accountable to their children for their responsibility in providing for and teaching them. Employed persons are accountable to their employers. Employers are accountable to the government. Government is accountable to the electorate. There is no way to live without responsibility of some kind.

Persons with integrity accept that fact and willingly and publicly acknowledge their accountability. They answer easily and truthfully to anyone who questions their actions, decisions, or motives. They are prepared to make full disclosure of their dealings and finances – to those to whom such disclosure is due. Because they know they are accountable for their attitudes and actions, they will always be dependable and trustworthy in everything for which they are responsible.

Imaginative

Imagination is an essential attribute of Christian leaders. They need to be able to see into the future through God's revelation and to set goals for their lives that will match that vision. Sharing the vision of God for their world – a vision revealed in both Creation and New Creation – enables leaders to provide the best possible guidance to those under their influence.

Imaginative persons allow God to give them the thoughts, ideas, dreams and visions that will motivate them to new heights of accomplishment. The motivation they receive will benefit many other people because God always moves us in the direction of doing those things that are best for everyone involved.

Tenacious

Leaders must be flexible; but they must also be inflexible, depending on the situation or the issue. We cannot be flexible all the time or we never will be committed to anything. Neither can we be inflexible always or we will be closed to new ideas and methods. Both flexibility and inflexibility are required of leaders.

As Christians, there are times when we must be inflexible and tenacious, holding on to what we know to be right, despite all the obstacles we face. If we have put our faith in God through Jesus Christ, if we are committed to doing God's revealed will, if we have received God's vision and plan and are interested in fulfilling His command in order to help the greatest number of people possible – in that situation, we must be fully committed, tenacious, purposeful, persistent, resolute, tough and determined. We must be just plain stubborn. But we must be careful that it is a divine stubbornness, rooted in the divine will. When we are sure we are in that perfect will, then we must cling to it and not turn loose.

Youthful

Leaders must be youthful. The mark of youth is the ability to look to the future with hope. Youthful persons are always budding, blooming, vigorous, active and strong. This describes the kind of persons we need to train in the Church to become leaders in the world. Especially in this generation of transition for the world, when the future is clouded and so uncertain for us all, we need leaders who are youthful in outlook and attitude.

All of the above words can be used to describe *Jesus Christ.* He was a man of integrity. He was a leader. He was mature and responsible and ready to take the initiative among his peers to make decisions that would benefit the greatest number of people. He was able to do that, in part, because *He had a healthy self-esteem.*

As we consider these words that are suggested by the letters in the word *self-esteem,* we want to consider how they relate to Jesus Who is our example for leadership.

Self-Esteem

Sincere

Jesus was honest and candid with everyone he met. He was sincere. He made no pretense about what people were like, alternately forgiving the sinner and castigating the self-righteous. He was plain and simple, straightforward in His relationships with others. People knew where they stood with Him.

Leaders are sincere persons. They are truthful, frank, unaffected and undisguised in their relationships with other people. It is not necessary to guess about what they are thinking. They are open and honest. They make their intentions and motives clear.

Eager

In the New Testament Gospels, we find many accounts of incidents from Jesus' life. In all of them, one thing stands out: Jesus was eager to get on with the work that he had come to do. Once he started, when he was 30 years old, he let nothing deter Him from the attainment of their goals. he knew what he was supposed to be doing, and he pressed on with it until the end.

Leaders are eager persons. They, too, are anxious to get on with the work they have to do in life. They pursue with vigor the objectives God has given them. They are earnest, enthusiastic and intent on the work set out for each of them. They are glowing, burning, intense in their commitment, but they temper their eagerness with a realistic attitude toward sleep, meals, time with family and personal hobbies. They move on from year to year, always pressing toward the fulfilling of the goals and dreams which God has given them for this world.

Liberal

Jesus was liberal. He was generous with His love, compassion and friendship toward all who were sincere seekers after God. He withheld nothing from others if they were in need and came to Him for help. He often went out of His way just to talk with one person who needed Him.

If we are going to be leaders, we must be generous in giving ourselves to others. We must be willing to be liberal in expending our energy, time and other resources in helping those who are in need. We must channel our giving (whether time or money) so that the greatest number of people will benefit from it. But we must never be so committed to the needs of the many that we miss the opportunities to help the individual as well. We will be liberal and generous with all. We will be lavish with our love, unrestrained in our giving, open-handed in our dealings, free and unselfish in our relationships with others.

Faithful

One thing can be said about Jesus without hesitation: He was faithful. Faithful unto death. He was faithful to God and to the doing of the divine will. He was faithful to His friends and to His disciples, who were not faithful to Him at the crucial moment of His death. He was faithful to the life He was called to live.

Leaders must be faithful according to that example. They must be true, loyal, constant, honest, dependable, firm, unwavering and devoted to their friends, to their work and calling in life, and to God. These are the attributes we need to develop in the people we train for leadership in the next century. The Church will need them. And the world will need them.

Effective

Jesus was not only faithful, He was also effective. He did not have the attitude: "All I'm required to be is faithful; it doesn't matter if there are results." Instead, He knew that His life must bear "fruit," as He called it. He promised His disciples that if they continued with Him, they also would bear "much fruit" in their lives. They, too, would be effective. In fact, once He even said that they would be more effective than He was. But He was effective in that He did what He set out to do.

Capable, competent, useful, fruitful – these words describe an effective person. The effective person will be a leader, and a leader will be an effective person.

Persons who accomplish what they set out to do are successful and effective. They are leaders.

Sacrificial

There is no better word than this one to describe the life of Jesus Christ. In our language, Christ and sacrifice go together. Our Lord gave up His life for others. He died for all. He loved the whole world so much that He gave Himself up for it. He lived to die. He gave up all His divine power and authority to become a human being, and then, on the cross of Calvary, He gave up His human life. But His sacrifice had a purpose. It was not pointless or in vain. His death made it possible for God to bring all people back to Himself[6] and to forgive them.

Persons with healthy self-esteems are able to willingly deny themselves, to freely give up their rights, to surrender their time and possessions to others. That is sacrifice. And self-esteem precedes it. If we know that we are important, that we have value, that we have something to give, and that our giving of it will benefit a great many people, we are able to sacrifice willingly and freely. That is leadership at its core.

Temperate

Jesus was not always "meek and mild," as the saying goes. Sometimes He deliberately chose to go to an extreme to accomplish something important. Surely, His death on the cross would be considered extreme. His chasing the money-changers out of the temple was also extreme. But He was always temperate, restrained and

---

[6]Where appropriate grammar requires a pronoun to refer to God, I have used the masculine form. The neuter "It" does not fit the personhood of God. Using the feminine form exclusively does not agree with the scriptural or common theological understanding of the nature of the Divine Being. However, please see Chapter 2, Part III for my use of "Mother" for God.

self-controlled – even then. He knew what He was doing, why He was doing it and what He would gain from it for Himself and for other people. That's self-control.

Leaders must be temperate. They must have self-control. They must be reasonable, moderate, unruffled and self-restrained. They then can choose, at times, to go to an extreme in order to accomplish something significant and beneficial to others.

Empathetic

Jesus had great empathy for others. He understood them. He knew what was in their hearts. He displayed an uncanny ability to read their minds. His best friends were the poor, the social outcasts and the hard-working fishermen of the peasant district of Galilee. His time was spent more with the sick, the helpless, the destitute and the hungry multitudes than it was with the rich and educated. He understood other people. He felt what they felt. He identified with them in their hurting.

The kind of people we need as leaders in our world must be like Jesus. We have said that it is in the Church that we must prepare these persons for leadership. One of the best lessons we can teach them is the need for empathy. Persons with self-esteem will be empathetic. They will be understanding, compassionate and appreciative of other. They will be sensitive to their feelings, and have insight into their problems.

People who are fearful, bitter and down on themselves are hurting so badly (and have so little self-esteem) they are seldom able to assist others. But those who are at peace, who harbor no resentments, who feel good about themselves – those who have healthy self-esteems – are able to empathize with others and be a help to them.

Ethical

If Jesus was anything, He was ethical. Many of the world's ethical teachings are built on Jesus' words. Even the non-Christian, unbelieving, secular world is willing to accept the teachings of Jesus as a good foundation for ethics. They do not live by those words, perhaps, but they recognize their value. Jesus, however, did practice what He preached. He lived what He taught. His life, as well as His teaching, was ethical to the core.

We need people with sound ethics. Leaders are moral, virtuous, good, principled and honest. They are trustworthy. When they make decisions, other people know they will be good decisions, which will benefit the greatest number of people. They know they will make decisions that are right and good, in the fullest sense of these words.

Mature

Jesus was mature. He had an attitude and experience that enabled Him to respond to every situation with the seasoned insight of a responsible adult. He was able to make good, sound decisions. That is maturity. It comes from the wisdom that God gives. It also comes from experience and from sincere compassion and commitment. It has many sources, and it is an absolute necessity for a leader.

There are different levels of maturity, as we have noted, but the true leader – at any age – is a responsible, mature person.

Mature people are those who have a full-grown understanding of life. They are hardened and toughened by experience. They are fertile and productive in what they do. They are ready, fit and complete for everything that happens. They are seasoned and mellowed by experience so they react to every circumstance of life with reason and stability.

Meditate on this definition for a while. Be mature.

Summary

An essential part of education in the Church (Christian Education) is the preparing of persons to be leaders in the world. We must train our people, young and old alike, to be mature, responsible persons who will take the initative among their peers to make good, positive, effective decisions.

Such persons will have *integrity*. They will be:

Individuals

Natural

Trustworthy

Energetic

Growing

Responsible

Imaginative

Tenacious

Youthful.

They will also have *self-esteem*. They will be:

Sincere

Eager

Liberal

Faithful

Effective

Sacrificial

Temperate

Empathetic

Ethical

Mature.

Such persons will be *leaders*. Will your church pre-pare the next generation of Christians to be leaders in tomorrow's world? Will *you* be a leader?

2

"Playing Catch-Up"

Christian thought has a history of "playing catch-up" with secular thinking. Through the centuries, particularly in the modern era (about 1750 to the present), most of the theology and practice of the churches has lagged a generation or two behind what has been happening in the world.

For instance, the concerns of this book – self-esteem and leadership – have been focal points since the 1950s for other disciplines such as psychology, sociology and business management. The ideas have been explored, the theories tested, and the initial results of putting them into practice made available for evaluation. Visit any library or browse in any bookstore, and you will find numerous books on both subjects. But nearly all of them have been written from a secular perspective.

In the churches, many people have been afraid to even discuss the issue of self-esteem, except to condemn it as somehow un-Christian. Any emphasis on the self, some have argued, takes away from God's glory. Or, some contend, we are to die to anything having to do with the self and live only to God. So, self-esteem as a positive, desirable trait for the Christian has been dismissed as inappropriate to the Christian life.

The same thing has been true of leadership, to some extent. We are called to follow Jesus, people have said, not men; and that is true, of course. We are called to be a body, and each of us members, with Christ only as the Head. Therefore, no one should be thought of as leading the others. Or so the thinking goes. As for Christians being leaders in the world – we are often reminded that we are called to be separate from the world. And, besides, the world is coming to an end shortly with the return of Christ, it is noted; so there is no future for the world anyway. And on and on go the arguments against including self-esteem and leadership among the important issues in Christian theology and practice.

But in recent years, the Church has started "playing catch-up" again. In most Christian bookstores now, you can find a few books on self-esteem and leadership in the secular world. A few. The subjects are still dismissed by many as insignificant issues. We are, after all, supposed to be concerned about the salvation of the world and not about social or political issues that demand leadership.

But the mood is changing. There is an openness now. Here and there, a few people are beginning to realize that these are vital issues – matters of life and death for our world. The Church needs to prepare people to be leaders in our world, people with healthy self-esteem who will be mature, responsible persons who will take the initiative in decision-making among their peers.

The future of our world depends on it. Significant issues are being decided in our generation, issues that cry out for such leadership. Among other things, we are making decisions regarding:

- nuclear disarmament
- abortion and euthanasia

- the nature of the family, including the questions of homosexual partners, unmarried partners, single parents, and the rights of minors

- the role of the Church and religion in society

- the distribution of the world's resources in a fair and equitable manner among the underdeveloped nations.

We dare not allow these decisions to be made only by non-believing, secular leaders. The Church must become involved in world affairs. If it fails to provide leadership for this crucial era, it will have abdicated its responsibility as God's stewards of the earth and as ministers of His reconcilation.

Those who are preparing leaders from a strictly secular perspective, however, are doing a good job, as far as they go. Before we delve into the implications of these issues for Christian theology, we could benefit from a quick survey of what some are saying in a secular discipline. Much work has been done in the area of business management. There are some important books on self-esteem and leadership in this field. To provide some guidance for our own thinking, and some background for comparison later on, I would like to share with you now some gleanings from several recent books which can be found in almost any bookstore.

* * * * * * * *

This first book was on *The New York Times* bestseller list for 12 months. *The One Minute Manager*, by Kenneth Blanchard and Spencer Johnson, spells out in easy language some of the basic principles of self-esteem and leadership. One of these principles is: "People who feel good about themselves produce good results." (p. 19.)

Another important principle is this: "Help people reach their full potential – catch them doing something right." (p. 39.) Praise them for it, the authors say. Let them know they are doing something right, and that you have noticed it. If you catch them doing something wrong, let them know that too – in no uncertain terms. But then follow through with what these writers call "the second half of the reprimand":

- shake hands, or touch them in a way that lets them know you are honestly on their side

- remind them how much you value them

- reaffirm that you think well of them, but not of their performance in this situation

- realize that when the reprimand is over, it's over. (p. 59.)

And then, say these experts in human relations, remember this last point: "Everyone is a potential winner; some people are disguised as losers; don't let their appearances fool you." (p. 71.)

* * * * * * * *

A second book, aimed at business executives, has a catchy title: *What They Don't Teach You at Harvard Business School.* It was written by Mark H. McCormack, a big name in the sports management and marketing industry. It is a practical book, filled with a lot of ideas that are not always appropriate from a Christian perspective. But one bit of advice from McCormack is related to this issue of self-esteem:

Make Them Feel That They Are Important –

It is very important to build employees up, make them feel important, and let them get credit for things that they have accomplished. It is important that you give them this credit directly and openly to their peers and to the outside world. (p. 194.)

* * * * * * * *

The third book was written by Harold Geneen, one of the top executives at ITT since 1959. It is called simply *Managing*. Geneen has not been known as a Christian businessman. I would not recommend all of his tactics and business practices. But he has some important things to say about the issue of leadership. One basic observation is as follows:

It has always been my contention that no one has a corner on brains. The greatest feats in business, as in virtually all of life, are performed by very ordinary, normal men and women. Not geniuses. Peak experiences of ordinary, normal people create leaders in business and elsewhere. (preface, p. x.)

And a related observation made later in the book is that "leadership cannot be taught. It can only be learned." (p. 127.)

This statement is true. Teaching "leadership skills" to people in the churches won't prepare leaders. We cannot train leaders the way a trade school trains mechanics.

Leadership preparation consists in helping people discover a new life, a quality of life that will enable them to face those "peak experiences" with faith, courage, hope, trust, integrity, and self-esteem. Such people will be leaders.

Geneen probably didn't mean this statement in the Christian context, but he did say it: "The ability to lead and inspire others is far more instinctual than premeditated and it is acquired somehow through the experiences of one's everyday life, and the ultimate nature and quality of that leadership comes out of the innate character and personality of the leader himself." (p. 128.) This observation becomes especially true when we consider who we can become as part of the New Creation in Christ.

Christian leadership education is a matter of instilling Christian character and personality.

* * * * * * * *

The next book brings us back to the issue of self-esteem. (Of course, leadership and self-esteem are inter-related. We cannot consider one without the other.) John J. McCarthy wrote a book called *Why managers fail . . . and what to do about it.* Among other causes of the failure of some managers is their lack of understanding of the importance of the individual employee. Consider some of McCarthy's statements on this subject:

> Every one of your people is a unique individual. (p. 37.)

> Working through individuals produces maximum productivity because each person can be motivated to produce his best efforts, simply because the benefits the manager men-

tions enhance the individual's self-image, and are responsive to his or her psychic needs, goals, and long-range objectives. (p. 39.)

Your purpose is to help the employee! How can you really help that employee unless you know what he or she desires out of life? (p. 42.)

You, I, and every person we know all want recognition, and there is no form more gratifying than the recognition by others of our intellectual growth, potential, and competence! (p. 49.)

Building self-esteem in other employees is important for any successful manager. And for those of us who are concerned about preparing people to be leaders themselves, building self-esteem is absolutely essential.

* * * * * * * *

One of the most important books recently published in this area is by Thomas J. Peters and Robert H. Waterman, Jr.: *In Search of Excellence.* The intertwining themes of self-esteem and leadership run throughout the fascinating chapters of this book, the subtitle of which is: *Lessons from America's Best-Run Companies.* Here is the accumulated wisdom of the best minds and most experienced leaders in American business.

Peters and Waterman studied in detail some of the nation's best companies in an attempt to isolate the factors that made them so successful. They boiled down the results to eight basic principles for running a successful company. I heartily recommend the whole book; but for our purposes, let me share, in their words, some of what these men learned about our twin issues:

> Attention to employees, not work conditions per se, has the dominant impact on productivity. (p. 6.)

> Among our early contacts were managers from long-term top-performing companies . . . . We heard talk of organizational cultures, the family feeling, small is beautiful, simplicity rather than complexity, hoopla associated with quality products. In short, we found the obvious, that the individual human being still counts. (p. 8.)

> So much of excellence in performance has to do with people's being motivated by compelling, simple – even beautiful – values. (p. 37.)

> We desperately need meaning in our lives and will sacrifice a great deal to institutions that will provide meaning for us. We simultaneously need independence, to feel as though we are in charge of our destinies, and to have the ability to stick out. (p. 56.)

> The excellent companies...provide an opportunity to be the best, a context for the pursuit of quality and excellence. They offer support – more, celebration; they use small, intimate units...and they provide within protected settings opportunities to stand out. (p. 60.)

The excellent companies are the way they are because they are organized to obtain extraordinary effort from ordinary human beings. (p. 81.)

...and, finally, these suggestions...

Treat people as adults. Treat them as partners; treat them with dignity; treat them with respect....There was hardly a more pervasive theme in the excellent companies than respect for the individual....These companies give people control over their destinies; they make meaning for people. They turn the average Joe and the average Jane into winners. They let, even insist that, people stick out. They accentuate the positive. Let me make clear one final prefatory point. We are not talking about mollycoddling. We are talking about tough-minded respect for the individual and the willingness to train him, to set reasonable and clear expectations for him, and to grant him practical autonomy to step out and contribute directly to his job. (pp. 238-39; emphasis mine.)

Here, then, are some of the *keys to leadership preparation:*

Attention to the individual

Compelling values

Meaning in life

Independence

Opportunity

Celebration

Support

Encouragement

Challenge

There is much more in this book about *excellence*. I encourage you to read it through and learn from it as you pursue the preparation of leaders in your church.

✳ ✳ ✳ ✳ ✳ ✳ ✳

Another fascinating book on leadership is one by Michael Maccoby: *The Leader: A New Face for American Management.* He examines six working leaders, from a foreman to a chief executive officer. He offers us some positive suggestions for leadership preparation. He recommends a style of leadership which he calls "the developer":

> The developers are oriented to human development....They clarify...goals they are asking others to accept. They invite participation in developing new ideas and they encourage subordinates to share power....Developers also demonstrate a leadership style that builds relationships and inspires trust....For those of us who are not at the top, we must recognize that there are leadership functions at all levels. (From the preface, pp. xv-xvi; emphasis mine.)

As one example of this style of leadership, Maccoby describes the work of Paul Reaves, who in 1973 "was the only black foreman at the Harman auto parts factory in Bolivar, Tennessee, where half of the workers are black"

(p. 66.). When he started that job, Reaves was "excited by the chance to practice a managerial philosophy of 'developing employees to their fullest potential.'" (p. 69.) Maccoby says that Reaves "gained authority because the workers trusted him; he cared about them and their development." (p. 75.) Reaves has had his tough times; but he "will not submit to defeat and despair...(because) he has learned that people need help, encouragement, and above all appreciation." (p. 81.) Maccoby expresses some of Reaves' thinking:

> Courage implies conviction. It may mean risking deep pain – contempt, rejection, loneliness – by expressing the truth to another person....In this sense, courage of the heart is related to both the intimate and the political, to both love and moral conviction....The exercise or development of the heart is that of experiencing, thinking critically, willing, and acting, so as to overcome egocentrism and to share passion with other people (justice-compassion) and respond to their need with the help one can give (benevolence-responsibility). The goal, a developed heart, implies integrity, a spiritual center, a sense of "I" not motivated by greed or fear, but by love of life, adventure, and fellow feeling. Reaves believes he will develop himself by service to others. (p. 88.)

When Maccoby has finished his detailed analysis of each leader whom he studied, he summarizes the characteristics that are common to them all. These *common traits of leaders*, from a secular perspective, can easily fit into a Christian perspective of leadership. Real leaders have:

- A caring, respectful and responsible attitude

- Flexibility about people and organizational structure

- The willingness to share power.

In addition to these character traits, effective leaders:

- Care about people and identify with their strivings for dignity and self-development

- Question whether the mission of their organization serves society and individuals

- Don't try to control everyone

- Spend more time up front developing consensus, but spend less time reacting to mistakes and misunderstandings

- Can give away power and let others share the functions of leadership without becoming insecure.

And, finally, it should be noted that effective leaders are:

- Flexible, competent managers with a sense of reality and...a sense of humor

- Not willing to gain power or money by going along with unethical practice or by pandering to the worst in people

- Secure enough to invite criticism and not afraid to defend an unpopular position

- Able to assert authority on issues of principle.

Here is Maccoby's summary: "With a new model of leadership, our values of freedom, informality, voluntary cooperation, individual achievement, and self-development can be the basis of more creative, innovative organizations." (pp. 220-228.)

* * * * * * * *

One final book on leadership introduces an idea which I would like to elaborate on later in this book: transforming leadership. James MacGregor Burns is the author of this Pulitzer Prize-winning book entitled *Leadership*. Here is what Burns has to say about *transforming leadership*:

> The transforming leader looks for potential motives in followers, seeks to satisfy higher needs, and engages the full person of the follower. The result of transforming leadership is a relationship of mutual stimulation and elevation that converts followers into leaders and may convert leaders into moral agents....Such leadership occurs when one or more persons engage with others in such a way that leaders and followers raise one another to higher levels of motivation and morality....Transforming leadership ultimately becomes moral in that it raises the level of human conduct and ethical aspiration of both leader and led, and thus has a transforming effect on both....Transcending leadership is dynamic leadership in the sense that the leaders throw themselves into a relationship with followers who will feel "elevated" by it and often become more active

themselves, *thereby creating new cadres of leaders.* (pp. 4,20; emphasis mine.)

Isn't this what leadership education in the Church should be all about? We are concerned with preparing all persons, if possible, to become leaders. We are not interested in separating leaders from followers. We want to help all people to become the persons God intended them to be and thereby to become leaders in the world. Their lives will be transformed, and, as a consequence, will then help to transform the lives of others.

As Burns thoroughly explored the sociological implications of leadership, he concluded that *self-esteem is one of the most powerful influences in determining whether a person will be a leader.* He defines *self-esteem* as "a high individual valuation of one's own worth." (pp. 94,95.) And he discusses the need for "the purposeful building of...self-esteem in order to enhance leadership potential." (p. 100.) And how do we build that self-esteem in others? By helping them develop "their capacity to learn":

> That capacity calls for an ability to listen and be guided by others without being threatened by them, to be dependent on others but not overly dependent, to judge other persons with both affection and discrimination, to possess enough autonomy to be creative without rejecting the external influences that make for growth and relevance. Self-actualization ultimately means the ability to lead by being led. (p. 117.)

In order to prepare persons to be leaders, we need to build their self-esteem. Or, perhaps more correctly, we need to help them develop their own self-esteem. That is a vital part of the teaching of leadership – if leadership can actually be taught. In response to the question of whether it can be taught, Burns says:

> We have conceived of leadership in these pages as the tapping of existing and potential motive and power bases of followers by leaders, for the purpose of achieving intended change. We conceive of education in essentially the same terms. So viewed, education is not merely the shaping of values, the imparting of "facts" or the teaching of skills, indispensable though these are; it is the total teaching and learning process operating...in the total environment, and involving influences over persons' selves and their opportunities and their destinies, not just their minds. Persons are taught by shared experiences and interacting motivations....Ultimately education and leadership shade into each other to become almost inseparable. (p. 448.)

This kind of living together and learning from each other in all that we are and all we do seems to me to be just the kind of educational process and leadership preparation that should be going in our churches. It is just this kind of leadership education, centered on the building of self-esteem, that is the focus of this book.

When we have begun to follow this pattern over a period of years in our churches, and when our children have begun to go out as adults, trained in this way to be leaders in the world, what will be the test of our success?

How will we know that we have prepared our youth for effective leadership in tomorrow's world? I can find no better answer to these questions than this statement by Burns:

> The ultimate test of practical leadership is the realization of intended, real change that meets people's enduring needs. (p. 461; emphasis mine)

3

Think About It

My wife and I have two teenagers. In listening to them and their peers, I have noticed that they commonly use a phrase which seems strangely appropriate in this context: "Think about it!" Now, as used by some teens, that expression is often intended as a disrespectful retort. But, in regard to the subject of leadership/self-esteem, I would like to encourage you, in the most respectful way possible, to *think about it!*

Think about what the world will be like 35 years from now. Every generation has had trouble projecting its thinking into the future. Most of us live as if we are part of the last generation which will ever walk the earth, with no thought given to succeeding generations. Many generations have felt that way. Yet there have always been successors. The world has not yet come to an end, though many groups (especially some Christian groups) have prophesied the end many times over.

As we approach the end of a millennium, many "prophets" are proclaiming that our world will never see the year 2000.

"Things cannot go on as they are," they pronounce with absolute finality. "All the prophecies have been fulfilled; the time is right for Christ's Second Coming. Our generation will be the last."

Perhaps they're right. But what if they aren't? What if the world goes on? What if the year 2001 arrives on the scene and the churches are still here, families are still struggling, people are still hurting, and nations are still fighting for survival? What then?

What if *you* are still alive and working and enjoying (or enduring) life in the year 2020, for example? If I am, I will be 72 years old. I hope to still be going strong then. My wife is the same age as I. Our children will be 50, 49, 47 and 42 – right at the prime of their lives. I don't think we can ignore the future and assume that it will never come, or (if it does) hope that it will go away. I believe we need to prepare now for tomorrow. We must be ready for it when it comes.

The Church needs to think ahead toward what its work will be like in another generation. For instance, in the year 2020, we may well have several operating space stations. They will need religious services, chapels, and chaplains; if they are large enough, they may even need churches for congregations of Christians who will be living and working there.

Thirty-five years from now, what will be the needs of today's "undeveloped nations"? Or will we have solved that crucial problem? Will we have learned to divide up the earth's resources in a fair and equitable manner so that all nations will have enough? (Somehow, even I think that is a bit utopian.) If we haven't solved these problems, how will we be dealing with them then?

For one thing, the Church will need to have moved from a rural mentality (which is the norm for most of American Protestant Christianity today) to an urban mind-set. We will need to have adjusted our thinking and practices to the needs of urban residents. We may no longer be locked into Sunday morning worship services, a mid-week prayer meeting, a Sunday school (before or during the regular church service) and a few dinners or socials from time to time throughout the year. The needs of hurting people will demand that the churches change their ways of ministry. The 24-hour-a-day schedules of our future urban societies will demand that we offer services and activities at all hours throughout the day and week.

Even today, the Church needs to think about providing leadership in what we have called the "secular" world. The fact is that it is our world, the one in which all of us live – Christian and non-Christian alike. Society is not divided into "us" and "them." It's just "us." It must be that way. We can no longer think that Christians can somehow live separate from the rest of the world around us. Rather, we need to prepare ourselves to assume the vital role of leadership our shared world needs now, and will need in the future.

Our churches must begin today to prepare those who will be tomorrow's teachers, politicians, doctors, corporate executives, industry foremen, research scientists, heads of government, journalists, media writers, producers and executives. We need to stop blaming "them" for our troubles, and start taking the initiative among our peers to do something about the situations in which we find ourselves today – and which we will have to face tomorrow.

I don't know what the future holds. I don't know all the answers about how the Church needs to change in order to be ready for the challenges of the future. If I did, I would write a book about it and become rich. No one knows. That's why it is so vital that we begin now to prepare as many persons as possible to become leaders wherever they are. We need many people who are fully prepared to lead others, those who will be on the job tomorrow in the government offices, in the media and business suites, in the board meetings behind closed doors where important decisions will be made that will affect the lives of countless numbers of people. It is these people – prepared by the Church to be leaders in the world – who will decide what needs to be done tomorrow.

The Care of the Body

Body-building has become a major hobby and business in America in the 1980s. People – both men and women – want to build up their muscles so they can show off their strength and the athletically-fit lines of their bodies. The image they present is of those who are ready and fit for anything.

In a different way, the Church needs to get into body-building. The New Testament describes the Church as a body, with each Christian a member of that body. Some of us believers are like hands, some like arms, some feet, some legs, some eyes and ears, and so on. Each one of us is vital to the proper, effective functioning and health of this body called the Church.

Any body which loses a hand or an eye or a leg is impaired to some extent. The loss, atrophy or weakening of any member will handicap the entire body. It is the same way with the Church. Every person who claims the name of Christ – everyone who says, "I am a Christian" –

is vital to the proper functioning of the effective Church. Every one of us needs to be strengthened, properly cared for, protected and respected so the body will remain healthy and whole.

The proper care of each member of the body is the responsibility of the whole body. A body-builder doesn't tell his leg: "You go do your exercises now while I rest my arms." That is ridiculous. He goes to the equipment room and uses every part of his body, exercises every muscle, puts every bone and sinew and tendon to the test.

The Church, in the same way, has to work together, exercising every member as we all work together in the testing, stress and development of the different parts. When a weaker member of the body is made stronger, more fully prepared for the work it is designed to do, every other part of the body is able to function more successfully. In our churches, we must work to prepare every member, every person, for the test of tomorrow's work.

In leadership education, this commmitment to the total development of the entire body must be our attitude. We are not concerned with training just a few – the elite, those who seem to be more capable or more interested. We are concerned with every person in our churches: young and old, new Christians and long-time members, educated and untrained, mentally limited and intellectually gifted, healthy and handicapped. We cannot afford, for our own spiritual and emotional health, to overlook or neglect even one person. All of our members must be prepared to become leaders in tomorrow's world, mature and responsible (at their own particular level) and ready to take the initiative in decision-making among their peers.

These people will have integrity and self-esteem. They will know that they are important to the future of our world. They will feel good about themselves, knowing who they are in Christ and what their God-given life goals are. They will be controlled by a positive attitude, expecting to become the persons God intended them to be. Their attitude and outlook will help to change those of the people around them, so that slowly the world itself will change.

As Christians, disciples of Christ, we are out to change the world. We can settle for nothing less than total accomplishment of that goal. We are sent out by God as light into darkness and salt into raw meat.[1] We are sent as those who have been comforted, forgiven and reconciled to God so we can help others find the same comfort, forgiveness and reconciliation that is ours in Christ Jesus. As our lives have been changed through the grace of God and our faith in Christ, and as we have entered into the New Creation through the Spirit, so we want to be agents of change, transformers of lives, leaders in the world who will make the decisions that will provide the best life possible for as many people as possible.

Catch the vision: come change the world with us.

---

[1] See Matthew 5:13-16.

Part II:
Hear the Challenge

Introduction:

A Critique of *Self-Esteem: The New Reformation*

Dr. Robert H. Schuller is the founder and senior minister of the 10,000-member Crystal Cathedral in Garden Grove, California. Each week he preaches to the largest television congregation in the world. Since 1970 he has conducted his Institute for Successful Church Leadership, which through the years has involved thousands of church leaders. Dr. Schuller is well-qualified to speak to our concern of preparing people in the Church to be leaders in the world.

In the first section of this book, we saw that self-esteem is basic to theories of leadership for corporate growth. Theorists in the worlds of business, politics and education have recognized this truth. But in the world of the Church, our theorists – our theologians – have not been so perceptive.

In his book, *Self-Esteem: The New Reformation*, Dr. Schuller calls the Church to the task of re-examining and reforming our theology and practice by recognizing and responding to self-esteem as *the* basic human need. He asks us to think about theology in an entirely new way, to rethink our understanding of God's relationship with human beings from the perspective of the human need for self-esteem.

What Schuller says must be heard and considered. We may not agree with every statement he makes. We may disagree with some of his conclusions. But we dare not ignore or lightly dismiss his basic message:

> If we hope as a church to survive, we must learn to think and feel and talk as caring believers who are sincerely interested in understanding and meeting the deepest spiritual and emotional needs of the unbelievers. (p. 13.)

Schuller claims that the deepest need of the human race is for self-esteem, and that this need is rooted in our Christian doctrines of Creation and of Christ (His incarnation, crucifixion and resurrection). He also claims that the Gospel can and should be focused on this crucial need.

Let's listen to Schuller himself. In this section, we will ask him ten questions which will explore the central issues of his message to the Church. As much as possible, we will allow him to speak for himself, through verbatim quotations from his book.

1

Question: What is the central purpose of this book?

Schuller's basic motive is to discover the most effective way to communicate to unbelievers the good news of salvation in Christ. This desire controls all that he says in this book. It is his focus, the center of his thinking:

> My ministry has, for over thirty years, been a mission to the unbelievers....I have seen my calling as one that communicates spiritual reality to the unchurched who may not be ready to believe in God. (p. 12.)

Isn't this, in fact, the calling of the Church? Isn't this what we all should be doing?

Schuller distinguishes between a church and a mission: the church being people who are concerned for themselves as an ongoing institution, and the mission being people who are concerned for others outside of the institution. I don't think these terms should be mutually exclusive. The Church should be both church and mission; but as a means of focusing attention on our top priority, it is a helpful distinction.

If the Church continues to be concerned more for itself than for others, it will die. If it spends money and energy on building new structures for its own use, developing new theologies in its own language, arguing over its own narrow problems and maintaining its inner power structures, it will cease to exist. But if the Church will spend its money and energy to meet the physical, emotional, and spiritual needs of those outside itself, if it will learn to speak to these people in a language they can understand, if it will address itself to their problems and concerns, then it will live and grow and be a major force in the world of the next century. It will do so because many of those who are now outside the Church will come into it.

That's evangelism. That's mission. That's the building up of the Kingdom of God. Isn't that what the Church should be doing? Schuller certainly thinks so:

> I call upon the church to make a commitment to remodel itself until it becomes the best thing that ever happened to the human race. The church becomes the best friend for all people when we proclaim the Gospel of Faith – Hope – and Love which truly stimulates and sustains self-esteem. (p. 21.)

Another passage needs to be examined at length here:

> Secularism has swept across the world like a raging forest fire, consuming the culture that had its roots in Western civilization – a culture largely flowered from the faith of classical Judeo-Christianity.[1] It seems that most every aspect of Western culture has been ravaged by the conflagration, including art, music, lan-

---

[1] The Church must be concerned with more than Western culture, of course. Its theology of mission must allow for differences in the varied cultures of the world.

guage, theatre, marriage, and the family. All have been shaken to their foundations in the twentieth century while a thriving, prosperous secularism laughs at the dying, institutional church and scorns her values and ways. And while this is going on, the institutional church denominations gather for their annual synods and conventions and spend thousands of hours debating amendments to amendments and playing the game of religious institutionalism according to *Robert's Rules of Order*. In the process, they fail to articulate a singular, exciting plan to launch a successful offensive against its arch enemy – secularism. Where is the flaming faith that can be fanned to sweep the young generations who today are still in wombs and cribs and playpens? What is desperately need-ed is a positive and exciting theology of mission that can win the world in the next mil-lennium. (p. 29f.)

This "exciting theology of mission" is what Schuller proposes in this book. It is a theology built upon the human need for self-esteem. It is, for many, a new way of understanding our relationship to God in Christ. It is not a new doctrine, but a new perspective on the historical doc-trines of Creation and Christ, of sin and salvation, of hope and love.

We need to rethink the meanings of the words we use and their implications for our lives. For instance, Schuller tells us how he uses the word *gospel:*

The good news is that God has promised us that any person who wants salvation can have it. And when that happens, Jesus Christ will come into our lives and make a permanent alteration that will irreversibly, divinely trans-form our deepest character so that we shall never live a life of self-denigration which leads to decadence and depravity. Rather, our life will reflect beauty, glory, honor, and dignity. (p. 129.)

Schuller asks us to reform our language, to learn to rephrase our thoughts, to redefine our words, to revise the implications of our symbols and images. He calls us to a new reformation of how we understand and speak of the spiritual realities of Christ and salvation and the highest creation of God: human beings.

This reformation has nothing to do with whether others within the Church think we are teaching the right doctrines. Our purpose, as Schuller sees it, is that we must seek a more effective way to communicate the Gospel to those outside the Church:

The most significant question that an evangelist must ask is: How can we communi-cate in a way that will lead a person to accept Jesus Christ as Savior and Lord? (p. 158.)

This is the central purpose of his book.

2

Question: What kind
of new reformation is needed?

In the process of finding a more effective way to communicate the Gospel to unbelievers, we need to reform both the theology and the practices of the Church. This call to a new reformation is a part of the title of the book and is obviously central to an understanding of it. So what kind of reformation is Schuller speaking of? What needs to be reformed? And why?

Let's begin with the why of reformation:

> Today the sincere, Christian believer is a minority. So the church must be willing to die as a church and be born again as a mission. We cannot speak out with a "Thus saith the Lord" strategy when we are talking to people who couldn't care less about the Lord! We cannot start with "What does the text say?" if we're talking to persons who aren't about to affirm respect for or unquestioning obeisance to "the text." (p. 13.)

The 16th-century reformation of Luther and Calvin took place in a world that was professedly Christian. It was in a very real sense an inner-Church argument. It was a conflict between Christians within the confines of the Church. As long as we continue that reformation or a reaction against it, the Church will be irrelevant to the world.

A new reformation, as Schuller calls it, will remodel the Church as a mission to unbelievers, molding its thought and words to fit the needs of the unchurched. The question is no longer, "What do we think is correct doctrine?" The question now is, "How can we effectively communicate the Gospel to those who don't believe?"[1] And if that is the question, our other questions – the questions which theology seeks to answer – must change. The perceived needs of those with whom we seek to communicate must form the questions we answer in theology.

"The most important question facing the church," says Schuller, "is: 'What are the deepest needs felt by human beings?'" (p. 13.)

Schuller becomes very clear at this point: "Self-esteem...is the single greatest need facing the human race today." (p. 19.) It is not just the need most widely recognized by people. It is not just a need perceived as such by unbelievers. It is at the root of our spiritual condition:

> I am convinced that the deepest of all human needs is salvation from sin and hell. I see sin as all-pervasive in humanity, infecting all human behavior and polluting the social institutions and systems at every level.[2] The result of sin is death and hell....What do I mean

---

[1] This has been the central question of Christianity from the beginning. In fact, it was to answer this question that the New Testament was written. But many times the Church has neglected this issue and has too often concerned itself with divisive questions of doctrine.

[2] One major criticism of Schuller's theology has been what others perceive as his down-playing of the importance of sin and repentance. Perhaps the problem is a difference in the way he understands sin, which he defines here. (See also Chapter 4, pp. 53ff.)

by sin? Answer: Any human condition or act that robs God of glory by stripping one of his children of their right to divine dignity....(or) that deep lack of trust that separates me from God and leaves me with a sense of shame and unworthiness. (p. 14.)

We will discuss this topic in more detail later on. But for now, our purpose is to determine the need for reformation and the kind of reformation which Schuller advocates.

He commissioned George Gallup, Jr., to conduct a poll on the self-esteem of the American public today. The results are enlightening (and frightening) for the Church:

> In summary, the people with a positive self-esteem demonstrate the qualities of personal character that the church would happily point to with pride in the members that we develop within our institutions. Unfortunately, the poll makes undeniably clear that the churches do not contribute to the self-esteem of persons. Only 35 percent of Protestants interviewed reflected a strong self-esteem. Thirty-one percent of Catholics interviewed demonstrated a strong self-esteem. In the "other faiths" category, 40 percent of those interviewed demonstrated a strong self-esteem. Obviously, the church is missing the mark.

> Now, the poll makes it clear that people who view God as a personal, loving, and forgiving Being, and relate to Him in such a personal way, do develop a strong sense of self-esteem that is exceptionally high and healthy!

At the same time, the poll demonstrated that ritualistic attendance at typical church services and the formal recitation of prayers do not in themselves contribute to a positive self-esteem. The facts are clear. The church is failing at the deepest level to generate within human beings that quality of personality that can result in the kinds of persons that would make our world a safe and sane society. The church is in need of a real re-reformation! (pp. 17,18.)

In Chapter 1, Schuller poses nine questions which the Church ought to answer. Four of these are particularly challenging to me:

Do you know professing believers who lack the emotional and spiritual wholeness that a healthy Christian religion should produce?

If the gospel of Jesus Christ is the truth that we proclaim it to be, then why is the established church in Europe and America declining, and why is the world not rushing in to accept the "Good News"?

Can the human needs met by spreading secularism not be fulfilled more effectively by the gospel of Christ if it is rightly interpreted and proclaimed?

How can the worldwide body of believers be motivated to fulfill the great commission and begin to share with compassion for suffering souls worldwide?

Do you know the answers to these questions? They are the kinds of questions I have struggled with myself. Here is how Schuller responded to his own questions:

> All of the problems, pressures, and perils addressed in the preceding questions arise from a basic defect in much of modern Christianity. What is that basic flaw? I believe it is the failure to proclaim the gospel in a way that can satisfy every person's deepest need – one's spiritual hunger for glory. Rather than glorify God's highest creation – the human being – Christian liturgies, hymns, prayers, and scriptural interpretations have often insensitively and destructively offended the dignity of the person. The human ego has been labeled as the ultimate sin, when, in fact, it is the mark of the image of God within people. The ego has been understood as something that must be destroyed or annihilated, when, in reality, it is to be redeemed. (p. 31.)

Here, then, is the kind of reformation we need. One that will change the way we proclaim the Gospel. One that will change our "liturgies, hymns, prayers, and scriptural interpretations." One that will open the possibilities of redemption to the people of God. This reformation will not be satisfied with the reformulating of dogma, but will demand a thorough revitalization of the Church so that it will conform to the glory of God in Christ. It will change the Church into a mission to unbelievers *and* a church in which believers fully reflect the glory and dignity of God's children.

"And the result will be a faith that will bring glory
to the human race for the greater glory of God." (p. 39.)

3

Question: What does self-esteem have to do with theology?

We can only answer this question in the context of Schuller's book by using his definition of *self-esteem:*

> Self-esteem is the human hunger for the divine dignity that God intended to be our emotional birthright as children created in his image. (p. 15.)

Given this meaning, *self-esteem* is a profoundly theological term, for it encompasses God's glory, our creation in God's image, our failure to conform to the divine image and purpose, and the redemptive and reconciling work of Christ to restore us to that image.

Schuller chose to develop his theology of self-esteem by using the outline of the Lord's Prayer.[1] He worked backward by formulating what he saw as the theological presuppositions of Jesus' words. These he tied directly to basic emotional needs of human beings. Here is his introduction to this whole section:

> The Lord's Prayer clears the way for a healthy theology of self-esteem, for it deals with the classic negative emotions that destroy

---

[1] This outline is not a detailed exposition of the scriptural text, but one use of it as a foundation for what Schuller has to say. I think there are other scriptures that more clearly say the same things. But discussion of that topic would be another book.

our self-dignity. The Lord's Prayer offers Christ's positive solution from these six basic, negative emotions that infect and affect our self-worth:

1) Inferiority: "Our Father who art in heaven,

Hallowed be thy name."

2) Depression: "Thy kingdom come, Thy will be done,

On earth as it is in heaven."

3) Anxiety: "Give us this day our daily bread;"

4) Guilt: "And forgive us our debts,"

5) Resentment: "As we also have forgiven our debtors;"

6) Fear: "And lead us not into temptation,

But deliver us from evil." (pp. 48,49.)

Let's take a summary look, then, at each of these six chapters of this "theology of self-esteem."

1) In answer to our *inferiority*, Jesus taught us to pray: **...Our Father which art in heaven, Hallowed be thy name** (Matt. 6:9 KJV). Every human being has been created in the image of God; and every person is meant to be a child of our heavenly Father. Sin has separated the children from the Father; so these words show the need for and offer the promise of "reconciliation to the estranged Father-child relationship." (p. 52.)

Sin is lack of trust, says Schuller. Our lack of trust in God has separated us from our Father, but we remain His children. We need only to be reconciled to Him by our brother – God's Son – Jesus Christ. Because we are the estranged children of God – and because, as children of God, we share in the divine glory – we all experience a "hunger for glory."[2] This hunger for glory *is* our need for self-esteem; and that need is fulfilled when we are reconciled to God in Christ, as children brought back into the Father's home and back into the family.

2) The second negative emotion is *depression*, which is countered with these words: **Thy kingdom come. Thy will be done in earth, as it is in heaven** (Matt. 6:10 KJV). Schuller says that "in this sentence there rises a hope for every human being to discover the lost glory his heart desires." (p. 70.) Here the plan of God and our dreams converge – "the dream of an exciting kingdom controlled by the gracious will of a wonderful God." (p. 71.) When we realize that we can be part of the exciting, divine purpose of God in building a kingdom on earth where Christ will be in control, our depression is dispelled and life takes on a new meaning:

> When we pray, "Thy kingdom come," we are praying for the successful growth, the prospering enlargement, of the increase of the number of redeemed people, looking to the day when human beings will be inspired by kingdom persons to treat one another with respect and dignity regardless of race, religion, economic class, or politics. (p. 72.)

3) The third section counters *anxiety* with this petition, **Give us this day our daily bread** (Matt. 6:11 KJV). In my opinion, Schuller presses his concern for self-esteem

---

[2] It is not that we hunger for the glory that belongs to God alone, but that God has offered to share His glory with us. So we hunger only for the glory that rightfully belongs to us.

too far in this section (Chapter 6), as we will discuss a little later. But he does offer some sound words to us all about our daily needs:

> "Give us this day our daily bread." What does the word bread mean? Bread refers to life's basic needs. God doesn't promise that we will get the dessert, but he does promise that we will have the crust.[3] That which we must have, we will have. We need air to breathe, water to drink, and we must have a crust of bread to live. And so we must trust God for the crust. What we need, God will provide. When God gives us what we need, it seldom seems like such a noteworthy thing. The basic necessities of life are seldom flashy or flamboyant. What's showy about a crust of bread? Yet it is the very thing that sustains our life. (p. 80.)

Schuller carries this discussion further to say that our daily needs which God will satisfy include "the thought from God that says, 'Do not quit!,' for with his help we will see the possibility of victory in the toughest times." (p. 82.)

(4,5) The next two negative emotions to be countered are *guilt* and *resentment.* Jesus counters them with these words: **And forgive us our debts, as we** (also have) **forgive(n) our debtors** (Matt. 6:12 KJV). Here's how Schuller ties these two emotions into self-esteem:

---

[3] What about people who don't even have the crust? Millions of people are living in poverty and are homeless and starving. What about them? The Church's responsibility is to be God's agents in providing the crust, at least, for the hungry, needy people of our world and thereby become the means by which God keeps this promise.

There can be no self-esteem without eliminating resentment and guilt. Both resentment and guilt must be washed away in divine grace before we can really feel good about ourselves. Now let us discover how we can be purged of guilt and personally forgiven. How can we receive the forgiveness we need? How can we receive the forgiveness that will save our spirits from the demonic, demolishing, and devastating effect of our guilt? (p. 97.)

According to Schuller, the answer lies in three words: sin, salvation and repentance. (pp. 98-105.)

SIN: At a deep level, sin is self-rejection[4] with the result that we then reject God's grace, we reject his love, we reject his calling.

SALVATION: It means to be permanently lifted from sin...and shame to self-esteem and its God-glorifying human need-meeting, constructive, and creative consequences.[5]

REPENTANCE: Real repentance is a positive, dynamic and highly-motivated redirection of life from a guilt-induced fear and its consequent withdrawal from the divine call to a caring, risky trust which

[4] Self-rejection is rejection of the person God intended us to be – our true self. See Galatians 2:20: **I have been crucified with Christ and I no longer live, but Christ lives in me. The life I live in the body, I live by faith in the Son of God, who loved me and gave himself for me.** Notice how often the pronouns "I" and "me" are used in this verse. The true self is who we are in Christ.

[5] According to the Gospel, this salvation is eternal. That is, we are delivered from sin's consequences forever. We will never be held accountable for our sin. We are forgiven.

promises the hope of glory, for yourself
and your heavenly Father.

6) The last negative emotion Schuller discusses is
fear, which he deals with in two chapters. The first
response to fear is found in Jesus' words: **And lead us not
into temptation...**(Matt. 6:13a KJV). Schuller discusses the
temptation to reject the way of the cross, the way of self-
denial and sacrifice. Here are a few comments about this
way:

> Self-affirmation then is the pathway to
> self-denial.[6] "I am a worthy person. I have
> something to give, therefore I can succeed in
> service, and I dare to volunteer." This means
> there will be no self-denial without strong self-
> esteem. And self-denial is the daring
> commitment of your name, your reputation,
> your integrity, your ego, on the altar of God's
> call to service. Mark this, it is important: The
> greatest cross any person can carry is to risk
> sacrificing his or her ego by risking the embar-
> rassment of a public failure in the pursuit of
> some noble, honorable, God-inspired dream.
> That is positive self-denial. It is denying your
> ego the selfish protection from a possible
> humiliating failure that might occur if you tried
> to carry out the divine idea. No one is more
> vulnerable than the person who makes a public
> commitment before he or she can be assured of
> success....That fear of public rejection, I submit,
> is the ultimate selfishness. This retreat from the
> divine call is the exact opposite of the self-

[6] See my discussion of humility in Chapter 1, Part IV.

denial Christ's call to discipleship demands. Christ's call to self-denial, after all, is always a call to a commitment to do something creative and constructive. (pp. 116,117.)

The second response to fear is found in Jesus' words: **...but deliver us from evil...**(Matt. 6:13b KJV). Schuller sees fear at the very root of evil, so he can then say:

> When we pray, "Deliver us from evil," we are trusting to be delivered from fear and its violent effects in our lives, and from the sources and stimuli that give birth to our fears. We are also praying that we will be possessed by such a positive faith and love that we shall be immune to the negative, fear-generating, evil forces. And we are praying that we will be positive personalities that shall never cause fear to rise in the lives of others. (p. 124.)

And he continues:

> Fear is the real reason humanity rejects the unconditional saving grace of God.[7] Why? We feel too unworthy to accept unearned, unmerited forgiveness and pardon. And we are fearful of a holy God who, because he is holy, could not possibly pardon us. So, our fear turns into doubt, deference, dishonesty, and rebellion. (p. 126.)

To follow Schuller's thought out to its logical conclusion, then, we should pray for God to deliver us from

---

[7] See my discussion of love, based on 1 John, in Chapter 3, Part IV. See especially affirmation six.

fear by which He then delivers us from "doubt, deference, dishonesty, and rebellion" and causes us to accept "the unconditional saving grace of God."

Schuller has one more chapter in the second part of his book which explores the theological implications of self-esteem. He takes up the closing words of the traditional version of the Lord's Prayer: **...For thine is the kingdom, and the power, and the glory, for ever. Amen** (Matt. 6:13c KJV). This is a kind of summary chapter. He builds it around these three questions:

(1) What in the world is God trying to do?

Answer: "He's building his kingdom."

God is trying to build his kingdom by appealing to our unsatisfied hunger for self-esteem. He offers to save us from guilt and shame and insecurity and fear and boredom to a life of security, serenity, stimulation, and self-esteem! Here then is a theology of salvation that glorifies God, for it glorifies his children.... (p. 136.)

(2) How in the world does God hope to succeed?

Answer: "By his power."

God's power is Christ living in you and in me. God's power is in any person who becomes a Christian and is compelled by the love of Christ....How does God hope to build his kingdom?...I believe it is by converting persons like you and me from shame to security, from inferiority to a sense of significance, from purposeless to purposeful living. (pp. 138,140.)

(3) Why in the world does God bother about it?

Answer: "For his glory."

God's need for glory compels him to redeem his children from shame to glory. God's name is glorified when his children are living honorable and glorious lives....The Christian faith and life is a gospel designed to glorify human beings for the greater glory of God. (p. 140.)

4

Question: Doesn't this approach to theology put too much emphasis on human beings — and doesn't it minimize sin?

Schuller's answer to this question is an unqualified "no." In fact, he would say that historical doctrine has placed too little emphasis on the value of the human being and too much stress on sin as wrong actions or a depraved nature. But let's allow Schuller to answer this question in his own words, beginning with a discussion of sin:

> I am convinced that the deepest of all human need is salvation from sin and hell. I see sin as all-pervasive in humanity, infecting all human behavior and polluting the social institutions and systems at every level. The result of sin is death and hell. I perceive the agony of human distance from God and helplessness to be more profound than articulated by classical churchmen. (p. 14.)

Three complementary answers are given to his own question, "What do I mean by sin?" (p. 14.)

> 1. Any human condition or act that robs God of glory by stripping one of his children of their right to divine dignity.

2. That deep lack of trust that separates me from God and leaves me with a sense of shame and unworthiness.

3. Any act or thought that robs myself or another human being of his or her self-esteem.

Then he continues:

And what is "hell"? It is the loss of pride that naturally follows separation from God – the ultimate and unfailing source of our soul's sense of self-respect....A person is in hell when he has lost his self-esteem. Can you imagine any condition more tragic than to live life and eternity in shame?[1]

In the second part of his book, Schuller further discusses his doctrine of sin. In Chapter 4 he says that "the core of 'original sin,' that state in which we are all born, is lack of trust." (p. 65.) Adam was created in fellowship with God, but,

somehow Adam did not trust God's promise for fulfillment enough to obediently abstain from the forbidden fruit, and the immediate result was guilt. And what is guilt but an ugly loss of self-esteem? (p. 65.)

For Schuller, all of Adam's descendants have been born with that continuing lack of trust: "Every child is born nontrusting." (p. 65.)

---

[1] To me, this is a confusing definition of hell, which is described in scripture as separation from God for eternity. Our separation from God in this life due to sin is a foretaste of hell, perhaps. Still, Schuller's last question ("Can you imagine ...?") demands a negative answer.

Now let's consider Schuller's definition of salvation. If the core of sin is lack of trust, then it follows that to be saved is to be brought into a trusting relationship with God and thereby to be restored to fellowship with Him. "To be born again," says Schuller, "means that we must be changed from a negative to a positive self-image – from inferiority to self-esteem, from fear to love, from doubt to trust." (p. 68.)

In Chapter 7, he again discusses sin. Here he says that "the core of sin is a lack of self-esteem." (p. 98.) He goes on to say:

> ...at the deepest level the heart of sin is found in what it causes us to do to ourselves. The most serious sin is the one that causes me to say, "I am unworthy. I may have no claim to divine sonship if you examine me at my worst." For once a person believes he is an "unworthy sinner," it is doubtful if he can really honestly accept the saving grace God offers in Jesus Christ[2]

> At a deep level, sin is self-rejection with the result that we then reject God's grace, we reject his love, we reject his calling – his dream for our life, and we are incapable of believing in the providential possibilities God has for us. We miss the mark because we fail to achieve what we could and should. We continue to sin,

---

[2] I am aware that this statement is in direct opposition to traditional Christian understanding of sin and repentance, but I agree with it. I think it is in harmony with both scripture and human experience. And I think it underscores the need for a new reformation.

i.e., reflect the lack of faith which results in our ongoing rejection of the potentially God-glorifying opportunities before us. And our lives fail to glorify God. (pp. 98,99.)

In Schuller's understanding, the lack of trust with which we humans are born is the core of sin. We do not trust God, and so we are separated from Him. We do not trust ourselves, and so we rob ourselves of the life God created us for – a life filled with love, joy, service, success through sacrifice, and the fulfilling of our God-inspired dreams. We do not trust others; so we continue to treat them with dishonor and disrespect, thereby sinning against them, ourselves and God.

In God's Image

Let's go back now to the first part of our question: "Doesn't this approach to theology put too much emphasis on human beings...?" A key to Schuller's answer can be found in his words: "God is glorified when his children are honored." (p. 98.) To honor God's children is to glorify God. To emphasize the value of human beings is to give supreme honor to our Creator.

Schuller's theology is firmly rooted in a positive doctrine of Creation. He holds as a primary truth that we are created in the image of God. And he maintains that as a continuing truth – that not just Adam and Eve, but every human being, has been created in God's image. That divine image was not lost to us or destroyed by Adam's sin. Fellowship with God was lost, and we must be reconciled. Innocence was destroyed, and our sin must be forgiven. Trust was lost and must be restored. But the image of God remains intact.

Question: Doesn't this approach to theology put too much emphasis on human beings – and doesn't it minimize sin?

The implication of that truth is that we were created to be God's family – the children of God, our Father. That is our divine inheritance. Again, the inheritance may be lost to us through sin; indeed, we can claim it now only through Jesus Christ Who has reclaimed it on our behalf. Nevertheless, it is our inheritance – promised to us in the fact of our being. We were created to live with God forever as His family, to share in His glory and love for all eternity.

Our lack of trust – and all the sin that stems from that core – now deprives us of that relationship. But we hunger for it – a hunger for the glory that is our divine right. That hunger is our lack of self-esteem. The fulfillment of regaining our glory as the children of God through trust in Jesus Christ is self-esteem.

So all theology, Schuller proposes, can be built upon this foundation of self-esteem:

> No theological question is more important than this: "What is the human being that you care about him? or the children of human beings that you care about them?" (Heb. 2:6, translation mine). It is the question that finds its answer first in the Creation, and finally in the Incarnation, the Crucifixion, and the Resurrection of Jesus Christ. No theology will long last nor will it ever succeed unless it begins with and keeps its focus on satisfying every person's hunger for personal value. All of the problems facing the church will find healing answers if we start with and do not get distracted at any time from meeting every person's deepest need – his hunger for self-esteem, self-worth, and personal dignity. (p. 35.)

But why? Why focus on human beings to such an extent. Because, to quote again the central purpose of this book:

> If we hope as a church to survive, we must learn to think and feel and talk as caring believers who are sincerely interested in understanding and meeting the deepest spiritual and emotional needs of the unbelievers. (p. 13.)

5

Question: Is this theology of self-esteem a new system of doctrine?

Schuller does not really offer us a systematic theology. What he does is call us to consider a new focus for reformulating our historical doctrines. He proposes the human being – the traditional doctrine of man – as the starting point for theology:

> The crisis facing the church now is a crisis of theology that centers on the doctrine of the human being. The single most important question facing the world today is: What is this creature called the human being? (p. 35.)

The doctrine of the human being, as Schuller proposes it, is founded upon the doctrines of Creation and of Christ (His incarnation, crucifixion, and resurrection).

Schuller's doctrine of Creation is never developed at length anywhere in the book, so we will have to piece together what he says on this subject. We begin on page 16:

> Why is this need for self-esteem so all-consuming in individual behavior and so all-important? It is because we are made in the image of God! We were spiritually designed to enjoy the honor that befits a Prince of Heaven.

We lost that position and privilege when our first parents divorced themselves from the Creator God.

And this:

> Because the human being is created in the image of God, the will to dignity is the irreducible, psychological, and spiritual nucleus around which the life of the human soul revolves and evolves. The need for dignity, self-worth, self-respect, and self-esteem is the deepest of all human needs. (p. 34.)

Schuller evidently sees the fatherhood of God, which he says is taught by Jesus in the Lord's Prayer, as an extension of God's creation of us. That is, God gave us life as parents do their children; and, therefore, we are created to be the children of God. And so he says:

> We were born to soar. We are children of God. The tragedy is that too many human beings have never discovered their divine heritage, so they live like animals. "Our Father in heaven, honorable is your name." The Fatherhood of God offers a deep spiritual cure for the inferiority complex and lays the firm foundation for a solid spiritual self-esteem. (p. 60.)

The significance of creation for a doctrine of the human being, according to Schuller, is two-fold. First, we are created in the image of God to share in the divine honor and glory. Therefore, every human being should have the dignity, honor and self-esteem due to one who bears God's image. Second, we are created to be God's family – each of us is meant to be a child of God. That is our divine inheritance. We should claim it, enjoy it, and share it with all other human beings.

We have already considered the nature of sin, which forms the transition between Creation and Christ. Jesus Christ came to reconcile us to the intended state and purpose of our creation. That is necessary because of our sin. But sin is, at the core, a lack of trust. That lack of trust has resulted in a lack of self-esteem. The restoring of trust and self-esteem in human beings is therefore the essence of the work of Christ.

One of the first statements in this book which caught my attention was this one: "Jesus never called a person a sinner." (pp. 100,126.) This is an important statement for Schuller's Christology – his understanding of Christ. "Jesus never shamed himself or others," Schuller says. (p. 100.) Jesus came to restore in us a deep sense of trust and self-esteem which would rob sin of its power at its core. But religious leaders have often turned religion around to be exactly opposite of what God intended:

> Jesus never called a person a sinner. He vented his sternest rebuke upon whom? The harlot? No. Jesus told her, "Your sins are forgiven, go and sin no more." Was it the secular materialists caught up in their success-oriented culture? No. "Follow me," Jesus said to them, "and I will make you fishers of men." Then who were the objects of Christ's righteous rebukes? And why? They were the well-esteemed, well-established, leaders and lords of the religious institutions of their day. Why them? What did they do that was so evil? Nothing is more evil than the evil that parades under the banner of goodness: "The Devil comes as an angel of light" (2 Cor. 11:14, my

translation). Claiming to represent God with the self-anointed authority to speak the Word of God, these Pharisees and members of the religious courts established a set of regulations that were impossible to fulfill and were certain to generate continual guilt. The fear of punishment, the fear of divine rejection, the false sense of guilt, the lack of self-worth, were all propagated in the name of religion. If the Jewish establishment was guilty of that in Christ's day, and if Luther found the Roman Catholic Church guilty in his day, I find the Protestant church far from innocent in our history.

The gospel message is not only faulty, but potentially dangerous if it has to put a person down before it attempts to lift him up. I protest all proclamations of portended Christian messages that attack the dignity of the person of a sinner while attacking the sin. (pp. 126,127.)

What *did* Jesus come to do? What *was* the work of Christ? On pages 100-103 Schuller discusses his doctrine of Christ. Let me quote his statements and a few of his comments on this subject:

By the incarnation of Jesus Christ God honored the human race...The Incarnation was God's glorification of the human being.[1]

---

[1] Traditional Christian doctrine has said that the reason for the incarnation and crucifixion is our sinful nature. Christ had to come in human flesh to make a proper sacrifice for our sin when He died in that body. The emphasis has always been on our sinful nature as the *cause*. But a new reformation should emphasize the *result* of the incarnation and crucifixion, along the lines of what Schuller says here.

By his crucifixion Christ has placed God's value upon us....If the deepest curse of sin is what it does to our self-esteem, then the atoning power of the Cross is what it does to redeem our discarded self-worth.

By his resurrection Christ has given us the highest honor – the opportunity to do his work and take his place in the world. Now Christ honors us by commissioning us to be his ambassadors, his statesmen, in the world community....What greater honor could Christ bestow on the human race than to step aside and ask us to become his body (Eph. 5.30); his ambassadors (2 Cor. 5.20); his voice; his hands; his heart; his mind (1 Cor. 2.16).

Christ, then, is *our hope of glory.*

In his incarnation, Christ has honored the human race.

In his crucifixion, Christ has placed unlimited value on the human soul.

In his resurrection, Christ has passed on to the human race his own glorious ministry.

Schuller's doctrine of the human being, built upon these twin doctrines of Creation and Christ, deserves to be taken seriously. It is not fully developed; he doesn't pretend it is. But he offers a starting point for reforming the doctrine of man so that it will include all people and so it will generate the trust and self-esteem which Christ came to restore.

With this newly formed doctrine of the human being as a foundation, we can then discuss all of theology from a new perspective. This is Schuller's proposal:

> I suggest that sincere Christians and church-persons can find a theological launching point of universal agreement if they can agree on the universal right and uncompromising need of every person to be treated with great respect simply because he or she is a human being![2] The "Dignity of the Person" will then be the new theological bench mark! Is there not a strong possibility that most sincere Christians might agree on this as the starting point, the undebatable standard, the human ideal? I offer theology of self-esteem as a starting position which will hopefully generate a climate and control for respectful discussion and constructive response to the challenges faced by the church today. (p. 37.)

---

[2] This point of agreement can be shared by non-Christians as well. Secular disciplines, such as education, sociology, and psychology, also stress the importance of self-esteem. Some other religions and philosophies also stress the value of the human being. So this point seems to be one on which we might have "universal agreement."

6

Question: Does this theology put too much emphasis on the Gospels to the neglect of the rest of scripture?

Every theology must start some place. Every building has its foundation before the walls and roof are added. Everything that is built – cars, planes, ships, highways, bridges – has a model, a blueprint, a mold from which it is fashioned. Schuller offers the Lord's Prayer as a model, a foundation, for Christian theology. But he urges us to build upon that foundation.

As he points out, the 16th-century reformation "looked to the Book of Romans in the Bible for (its) primary inspiration." (p. 39.) He suggests that an interpretation of Paul's writings served as the blueprint of reformation theology. He thinks that the words and the "Spirit of Jesus Christ" would serve far better as a model for the construction of a new theology of self-esteem.

Specifically, Schuller uses the Lord's Prayer as a starting point to "discover a new theology, one that offers salvation from shame to self-esteem"...where "we shall discover that self-esteem rooted in Christ's love finally satisfies every person's thirst for glory." (p. 39.) He assumes that this prayer – a model prayer which Jesus taught His disciples to pray – reveals the central concerns of Christ.

What better model can we find, as a starting point, to discover and unfold the deep concerns of our Lord?

His concerns are our concerns, surely. If we strip away what is peripheral in the Gospels – indeed, in all the scriptures – and get to the heart of Christ Himself, would that not then serve as an ultimate authority for us? The question, after all, is one of authority. Who will decide – when there are differences – which interpretation is correct? When there seems to be key differences between what one writer of scripture and another has to say, to whom do we turn for an authoritative decision? Here is Schuller's answer:

> What, or who, will remake, renew, and reform us? What supreme authority will be the architect of our theological reconstruction? We cannot simply anoint self-esteem as our philosophical supreme authority unless it is in fact the centrifugal force in the mind and heart of Christ. If it is merely a humanly contrived apologetic, it cannot stand as a philosophical authority, for self-esteem will not be without its own unique contradictions. Christ must be Lord over the ultimate human value. Any theological suggestion that self-esteem is to be the bench mark of our theology loses integrity, authenticity, and must be branded as counterfeit and contrived secular humanism unless it is central to the concern of Christ. (pp. 44,45.)

But what is "central to the concern of Christ"? Schuller answers, again, that the Lord's Prayer reveals this central concern, and that a study of the prayer will give us a solid foundation for building a reformed theology of the human being. He does not suggest stopping there. In fact, I am sure he would urge us to then search all the texts of scripture to discover additional support for this theology. The question is not whether we use the Gospels or the Epistles or the Old Testament. It is whether we anchor our theology to Christ rather than to Paul, Moses or anyone else. I think we must agree with Schuller that we will accept Christ as our anchor and our authority.

7

Question: How can self-esteem and self-denial be reconciled?

Schuller answers this question in Chapter 5 of his book, which is entitled "The Divine Design for Human Dignity." Here is his summary thought on this subject:

> Self-affirmation and self-esteem inspire sacrifical service which generates fresh self-worth. I call this self-esteem recycled. (p. 71.)

Anyone who finishes this book and still thinks that self-esteem, as defined by Schuller, is selfishness or self-centeredness, has not understood what he has read. Self-esteem is the direct opposite of "self-service." Real self-esteem enables a person to be totally selfless in serving others.

True self-esteem, as we have noted, is rooted in total trust. When we trust God and ourselves, we can trust others and not be afraid they will dominate us or deprive us of something. We can be free to give, to share, to love, to be totally involved in serving others.

Schuller says that God's plan for us is to participate in the building up of His kingdom on earth – bringing people under the Lordship of Christ by fostering trust and self-esteem in them. This self-giving service is the "divine design" – "God's dream" – for our world. As Christians, we are called by God to dream with Him of a world of trusting people who are filled with sound self-esteem, people who are in a trusting relationship with God and with each other. What a dream. Here is what Schuller says about it:

> When God's dream is accepted, we must be prepared to pay a high price. The dream that comes from God calls us to fulfill his will by taking an active part in his kingdom. The price? A cross. The reward? A feeling of having done something beautiful for God! But the path will lead us through the valley of potential humiliation before the crown of godly pride is placed upon our heads. That in part is what the Cross means....There is no self-esteem without sacrifice. There is no sacrifice without being exposed to the possibility of ridicule. There's no way we can pursue a dream without running the risk of people saying, "Who does he think he is?" What separates dangerous egotism from healthy self-esteem? The difference is the cross we are willing to bear to fulfill God's will. The cross is the price we will have to pay to succeed, i.e., to realize the inspiring dream God has given us. (pp. 75,76.)

Don't dismiss this concept too easily. We are not talking here of self-centeredness, egotism, selfish pride or an "I'm Number One" mentality. We are talking about trust and healthy self-esteem which is anchored in the fact of who we are as the children of God, created in His image and reconciled in Christ to our true being. This self-esteem leads us to self-denial and sacrificial service as we dream with God of the kingdom which is being built up even now through Jesus Christ. We will trust God; we will trust ourselves; we will trust others. We will build up the self-esteem of others knowing that our own self-esteem is thereby strengthened. We will give up our lives for the sake of this kingdom. Even more importantly, we will risk everything for the honoring of God's children and for the greater glory of God.

8

Question: How can success and sacrifice be compatible; doesn't one exclude the other?

Once again, we can discuss Schuller's proposals only if we use his definitions. Here's how he defines *success:*

> Success is experiencing the self-esteem that arises deep within us when we build it in others through sincere self-denial and sacrificial service. (p. 76.)[1]

So, to Schuller, success is *not* related to how much money we have, how often we win, what job we work at, where we live or any other such criterion usually used to measure it. Our success is judged exclusively, according to this definition, by the depth of self-esteem which is directly related to our self-denial and sacrificial service to others.

Success and sacrifice, then, are not only compatible, they are mutually inclusive. Sacrifice leads to success; success is a product of sacrifice. And both are built upon a solid self-esteem. Schuller goes on to say:

> God's ultimate objective is to turn you and me into self-confident persons. And only self-confident persons become leaders capable

---

[1] See Chapter 2, Part III for my definition and discussion of success.

of creating a self-esteeming society. Material things, of course, do not build self-confident persons. Self-esteem that is rooted in materialistic status symbols (we need not elaborate) has a short life span. Fashions change quickly, but self-confidence rooted in sincere and sacrificial service, in answer to God's Cross-centered call, is sure to bring ultimate satisfaction. (pp. 80,81.)

With this understanding in mind, Schuller discusses the problem of poverty. He says that "what is bad about poverty is that at its worst it leaves persons without any self-respect." (p. 81.) I agree with that statement. Poverty and self-esteem are seldom companions. But does that mean that only people with money can have self-esteem? Can't poor people have it as well? Wouldn't such a statement mean that, in fact, money is necessary for success, even according to Schuller's definition? At one point, he seems to say exactly as much:

> To fail to inspire persons to strive for financial security and ultimate financial independence leaves them vulnerable to any ambitious, politically power-hungry manipulator. After all, if I'm not encouraged to save and invest wisely my acquired money, I will be forever dependent on the state – on society – for the health, education, and welfare of myself and my family. The more dependent I am the less sense of freedom to be creative, the less self-esteem I can experience, the less joy of giving I can know. The poor cannot help the poor. (p. 114.)

Yet Schuller obviously objects to any materialistic idea of success. He agrees completely that material things are worthless in themselves. He makes it quite clear that just the giving of money to people – whether rich or poor – is no solution to their basic need for self-esteem.

The answer, he suggests, is "giving them thoughts before things." (p. 81.) We need "creative, inspiring, possibility-pregnant...God-inspired thoughts." (p. 82.)

God-given ideas will challenge and equip us to rise from poverty to pride. As we grasp the ideas, pursue the challenges, and realize success, we can discover the pride of earnership as well as the pride of ownership. (p. 83.)

In my opinion, this is the weakest part of Schuller's book. He wavers between saying that success is not to be measured in terms of material possessions or achievements and openly suggesting that, in fact, it is evidenced by these externals:

At the bottom of every ladder, there is a crowd of talented, trained people with academic degrees and credentials who can drop names and claim connections, but they aren't going anywhere. Really, success is not a matter of talent, training, or territory as much as it is the skillful and prayerful management of divinely-inspired ideas. The difference between the people at the top of the ladder and those at the middle and the bottom is so basic. The people at the top have learned how to handle good ideas, but those who stay in the middle or at the bottom of the ladder have never learned to hatch, harbor, and handle creative thoughts. (p. 85.)

In my estimation, the problem with Schuller's approach to success[2] is that it denies the possibility of success to those at the bottom of the ladder. Most people cannot, by the very nature of things, live high up the ladder. It is a sad fact that, no matter how much self-esteem we seek to generate in others, the majority of the inhabitants of this world will never have more than the basic necessities of life (if they even have that much). The building up of the kingdom of God cannot – and must not – be equated with the growth of bank accounts and build-

---

[2] It is hard to find direct statements in any of Schuller's books about the relationship between wealth and success. Contrary to what some people seem to think about his ideas, he does not consider money a key ingredient of success.

Here are two of his more direct statements from other books on this issue:

"Money, in and of itself, doesn't build real self-love....a youngster who...looks upon money as something he can use to help those in need and as something to educate and train himself and eventually his children, then it can become important in building self-love. For we love ourselves when we help others become what they should be. Money builds hospitals. Money pays for scientific research which will heal the sick. Money is important. Every person owes it to himself and to society to earn the most money possible in the best possible way if he uses it for a real contribution to society." (*Self-Love,* p. 116.)

"Success isn't measured by the money you accumulate. To be sure, since honest success is the result of meeting authentic human need, it often follows that Supersuccessful People become wealthy people. In a world that cries for money to eliminate poverty, ignorance, and disease, we may hope there will be many persons who acquire wealth in order to build a healthier and happier human community. But no matter how wealthy Supersuccessful People become, they never forget that "being" is more important then "getting." What you are is more important than what you have. I have a friend who has set a goal of making a million dollars in order to give it all away. Now that's a Supersuccessful Idea." (*Reach Out for New Life.* p. 14.)

ings or the climbing of the ladder of recognition and wealth.

Schuller does have some good things to say about a Christian response to poverty:

> Can we stand silent and indifferent to poverty? No, for it robs the poor of their pride as persons. Somehow we must support, inspire, or motivate the forces that can cause the poor to recover their dignity through development. (p. 139.)

What Schuller says about our usual approach to poverty is also true:

> What is bad about poverty is that at its worst it leaves persons without any self-respect. Real, abject poverty strips a human being of his dignity....And so we ask, how can we eliminate poverty in such a way that we eliminate the worst in poverty – loss of dignity? How do we replace the loss of self-esteem in the very poor with what they need most of all – dignity, self-esteem, self-confidence, noble achievement, pride of accomplishment, pride of ownership? This can happen by giving them thoughts before things....Too often the welfare check deprives people of dignity and makes them feel dependent....Consequently, what people need today, more than welfare checks or hand-outs, are thoughts – opportunity-revealing, possibility-thinking thoughts! (pp. 81,82.)

I believe this whole discussion needs to be revised[3] because it begins to slip back into a false sense of success, especially when viewed in light of Schuller's own definition of success:

> Success is experiencing the self-esteem that arises deep within us when we build it in others through sincere self-denial and sacrificial service. (p. 76.)

---

[3] I discuss this issue briefly in Chapter 2, Part II. However, most of what I say about self-esteem in the rest of my book focuses on the inner qualities of life. The issue of wealth is only indirectly related to self-esteem and leadership.

9

Question: In Part III,[1] aren't these "theologies" just different implications of theology?

The term *theology* is defined differently by various people. Schuller never defines it. So let me offer a definition we can use in this discussion: *Theology presents in a systematic way our understanding of the relationship between God and human beings.* Given this meaning, does Schuller's proposal in Part III of his book constitute the "full-orbed theological system" (p. 150) that he calls for?

At the center of his proposed system is what Schuller calls his "theology of self-esteem." Surrounding that center are five other "theologies": of evangelism, social ethics, economics, communications and mission. My question is whether these things constitute theology at all, or at least whether there are not other essential matters of theology left out of this system. Schuller includes within his theology of self-esteem a discussion of creation, salvation, sin and Christology, as we have seen throughout this book:

> This is, make no mistake, a theology of
> the salvation of the soul. Salvation is defined as
> rescue from shame to glory. It is salvation from
> guilt to pride, from fear to love, from distrust to

---

[1] Part III of Schuller's book.

faith, from hypocrisy to honesty. It is salvation "by grace through faith," and it is experienced when we encounter the Ideal One who accepts and does not reject us. Hence, the stronger the Christology, the richer the self-esteem; the stronger the sense of sin, the more glorious the joy of salvation and self-esteem. We were so bad, and yet Christ needs and wants us. (p. 151.)

Our understanding of Creation, Christ, sin, salvation, forgiveness – indeed of all the historical doctrines of the Christian faith – "begins with the truth that the human being is a glorious, dignified creature, with infinite value in the sight of God." (p. 151.) Christian theology revolves around and is integrated into that truth.

The focus of the book is clear: to urge us to reform our system of theology around this center of human dignity and self-esteem. Every part of the system would be tested against this standard. I think Schuller should be taken seriously on this issue. In the next section of my book, I will offer my own proposals for such a theology[2]

But my original question stands – aren't the other "theologies" (evangelism, social ethics, etc.) implications of a systematic theology which has human self-esteem at its center? Any theological system will include an understanding of how human beings are related to each other as

_____

[2] My proposals in this book are not systematic either. A full discussion would require other books. What I have done in Part III is focus on eight central aspects of the divine-human relationship (based on Genesis 1-3). If theology requires us to develop an understanding of the relationship between God and human beings, then this understanding can form the basis for a fuller systematic treatment of Christian theology.

well as to God. The responsibilities of those relationships should also be dealt with. It is in this context that such matters as economics and communications are involved.

The weakness of Schuller's diagram of his proposal (p. 150) is that God and eternity, for instance, are presented only as sub-headings under the main themes of human interaction. To me, such a theological concept is dangerous. I doubt that Schuller himself intends that it be taken literally. Still, we need to hear his basic call to reformation:

> So I contend and plead for a full-orbed theological system beginning with and based on a solid central core of religious truth – the dignity of man....I submit that an authentic theology of salvation which begins with the truth that the human being is a glorious, dignified creature, with infinite value in the sight of God, will produce a theological ladder that will stand on solid, immovable ground. (pp. 150,151.)

10

Question: How can this theology of self-esteem make a difference in preparing people in the Church to be leaders in the world?

Schuller's final chapter is strongest at this point. We need people who will lead the Church out into the world, fully prepared to lead not only the Church but the world as well. We need people who are convinced that they are the children of God and whose "hunger for glory" is fully satisfied in that knowledge. We need people who are trusting and, therefore, able to deny themselves and sacrificially serve others. We need people who know that success requires a deep self-esteem which is rooted in self-denial and sacrifice. We need people who have discovered their divine and eternal value in Jesus Christ and who want all the world to share in that discovery. Such people are the leaders which both the Church and the world desperately need.

These leaders will view the unconverted individual as "a nontrusting person – fearful and suspicious – instead of as an 'evil' or 'depraved' or 'shameful' soul." They will "visualize every person as precious and valued in God's sight with vast untapped possibilities of service to God and his fellow-man." (p. 156.) They will see the truth in what Schuller says about mission:

Real mission is meeting human needs. And in the process, we shall see secularism sold short by a bigger, better, and more beautiful idea – positive Christianity. We won't need to fight secular humanism; we simply offer a deeper, more desirable alternative. For no philosophy, no ideology, no theology can meet the deepest needs of human beings as attractively and pragmatically as a dynamic and dignity-instilling Christian theology of self-esteem. (p. 173.)

These leaders will practice social ethics, economics and communications with this goal in mind: "to treat all persons with the dignity they deserve as human beings." (p. 161.) Attacks against other persons – whether verbal, printed or physical – will not be tolerated. Manipulation or intimidation will find no support. Exploitation because of sex, race, age, or religion will be totally rejected. This dream is not utopia; it is the Kingdom of God.

People who have a self-esteem anchored in their trust in God, who know who they are as the children of God reconciled in Christ, who are ready to follow self-denial and sacrifice as the road to success – such people are the leaders which the Church and the world so desperately need.

Part III:
Develop an Understanding

1

Achieve Your Potential

This third section is an exploration into Christian theology. We need to develop a better understanding of our nature and potential as human beings. We can't fully develop this understanding outside of Christian theology. *Self-esteem* is a term used by other disciplines such as psychology, education and sociology. It has different meanings in different contexts. In the context of our discussion, self-esteem is related to who we are as human beings created by God – those who have the potential of the new creation in Christ.

Creation and New Creation, then, are the foundational concepts we need to grasp and understand. What were we created for? What is our created potential as human beings? Even though some of that purpose and potential was lost to us through our sin, God has restored it to us through the new creation in Christ. So to discover what we were created for is to discover what our potential is now that we are restored in Christ.

I call this discovery *Potentiality Thinking*. You have heard of positive thinking and possibility thinking. This approach is Potentiality Thinking. Realize what your potential is. Believe that you can achieve it. Then go after it through faith in Jesus Christ, knowing that you are part of the new creation. Potentiality Thinkers have an attitude of expecting to become the persons God intended them to be.

What creates self-esteem in us more than knowing how important we are and what fantastic potential we have? Once we come by faith into this new creation, we have a confidence, rooted in what God has done in Christ, that will generate positive self-esteem. This confidence makes us feel good about ourselves. And why shouldn't we? God loves us. In Christ, He has forgiven us. We have the Spirit of God living within us to empower us for this new life. We have a divine inheritance held in trust for us. We are the children of God, the divine family restored to its intended existence. So why shouldn't we feel good about ourselves? Why shouldn't we have abundant self-esteem?

Self-esteem will enable us to be responsible, mature human beings. We will not be controlled by others or led around by those who have not yet entered into their full potential. Instead, we will lead them. We will affect how the world lives and thinks by providing the example, teaching and guidance it needs to become what it was created to be. We will be the leaders of our society because we will have the confidence, generated in Christ, that gives us the courage and boldness to step out ahead of the crowd and lead the way into better things.

So this section is about leadership. It is about self-esteem. But from here on out, we will not use these terms very much. Instead, we will focus on the twin terms of *Creation* and *New Creation*. We will focus on *Potential* – what it is and how to achieve it.

You may be wondering how this approach relates to Christian theology. Let me restate the definition of theology offered in Part II: *Theology presents in a systematic way our understanding of the relationship between God and human beings.* I don't propose that this brief discussion will offer anything like a full system of theology. But we will touch on the basics. We will highlight what we need to understand concerning this relationship between God and human beings. We will take from the Creation story in Genesis eight basic characteristics of the created/newly created life which God has given us. These eight traits define our potential. The list is not exhaustive; but it is fairly complete, covering most of the concerns of daily living.

You may have been taught that any theological system must begin with God. I agree with Dr. Schuller that we need to reform our way of thinking to begin with human beings. If we are to have a theology that will speak to the needs of people so they will hear the Gospel and believe in Jesus Christ, we must begin "where they live." People want to know what their lives are all about. What is the point of our existence on this planet? What is our purpose in being here? What is our potential in life? As we answer these questions from a Biblical perspective, we will answer other theological questions as well (though we won't be able to go into them at length here). We will answer questions about what God is like, Who Jesus Christ is, what the work of the Holy Spirit is, what the place of the Church and the scriptures is in our lives.

This section is about Christian theology, but from a human-centered perspective. We need to understand the relationship between God and ourselves. In order to do that, we will develop our ideas around the terms of Creation and New Creation, beginning with what is stated or implied in Genesis and moving on to what the New Testament teaches. We will discover our potential in Christ and will discuss how we can achieve our full potential in life.

2

Set the Highest Goal

Our human potential is far greater than most of us ever dare to dream. Too often we limit ourselves to small dreams, to little visions, to mediocre projects. Few of us dare to think that we can do anything extraordinary with our lives. We have been taught that we are *only* human – and we have believed it. We have been trained to think that, as human beings, we have little significant potential.

We need to retrain our minds, to turn our thinking around, to understand the potential of our existence in a new way – which is really not a "new way" at all. The Creation account in Genesis 1-3 presents our created potential as something far more than we have ever dreamed.

The greatest book for expanding our understanding of who we can become is the Holy Bible. The place to begin reading it is at the beginning, in the ancient story of the creation. The Bible portrays people not as *only* human but as *fully* human. Read the Bible. Learn from it. Let it turn your thinking around as you begin to realize who you are in Christ, who you can be in this world and how far you can go in life.

The trouble with most plans for success is that they are too limited. They don't go far enough. They are only concerned with superficial things such as money, prestige, fame and power. They are built around outward accomplishments, things people can see and praise: "You're really something; look at what you have done with your life."

But is the greatest kind of success only our superficial, outward achievements? Isn't there more to life, to success, than the attainment of "all these things"?[1]

True success is the accomplishment of a goal or objective. We are successful if we accomplish what we set out to do. If a man decides to make a million dollars before he is 30 years old, and does so, then he is successful. If he sets the goal of becoming president of a corporation, and is selected to this position, then he is a success. If a woman says, "I'm going to be the top salesperson in my company this year," and does what she says, then she is successful.

But aren't there other, more worthy, goals in life? Aren't there goals that we can set for ourselves that go beyond the tangible evidence of bank accounts, top positions or public acclaim?

Our highest goal in life should match the highest purpose of our creation. To set that kind of goal we have to answer the basic questions of our existence: Why are we living? What meaning or purpose is there to our being here? Why were we created? When we have answered these questions, when we have determined the reason and purpose for our creation and existence, then we are ready to begin setting goals for our lives that really count. Once we have set such goals, success will then take on new meaning.

---

[1] In fact, if such things as money, prestige and power are the criteria for success, only a relatively few human beings can ever be successful. True success, as defined in this book, is available to every person.

If success is the fulfillment of goals, then the nature and quality of those goals determine the nature and quality of our success. If our goals are limited to the attainment of money and fame, then success will be nothing more than being rich and famous. What a small-minded, short-sighted goal for us (even if it were possible for all of us to attain, which it is not). But if our goals match the purposes of our creation, of our very existence, then *success means the achievement of the full potential of our divine creation.*

What, then, is our potential? What are the purposes of our creation, of our lives? What is the meaning of life? Why are we here?

These questions are answered for us in the creation account found in Genesis. Basically the answer to all of them is summed up in this one statement: *we were created to be like God.* [2]

> **Then God said, "Let us make man in our image, in our likeness, and let them rule...over all the earth...."**
>
> **So God created man in his own image, in the image of God he created him; male and female he created them.**
>
> **Genesis 1:26,27**

You and I were created to be like God – we were made in the divine image and likeness. That is our potential; that is the purpose of our existence. Why should we settle for anything less?

Here is a 3-D formula for successful living:

---

[2] We were not created to become gods nor to usurp the power or glory of God (see Gen. 3:5), but ...created to be like God in true righteousness and holiness (Eph. 4:24), and to Be imitators of God....(Eph. 5:1.)

Dream big.

Dare to be more than you ever thought you could be.

Do all you can with what you have where you are now so you can achieve your fullest potential.

In this book, we are focusing on leaders. If we are going to become – and train – leaders in this world, what better goal could we have than to become like God? If we are going to model ourselves after someone, then let's imitate the very best. There have been many great men and women who have been leaders in their fields, among their peers, and who have been remembered for centuries. But none of them can match God as an example for us to follow in our preparation for the achievement of great things.

The obvious question is, "How in the world can we humans be like God?" No one has ever seen God. We can't sit down and talk to our Creator, to examine the divine personality to determine what we should be like. If we are to be like God, how can we know what our Divine Model is like? What kind of character or personality should we have? What thoughts should we think? What words should we use? What actions should we take?

The answer is simple: one person in history has embodied all that God is and has shown us what God is like in order to give us a living model to follow. His name is Jesus of Nazareth. The Church has given Him the Jewish title of the Messiah, the Chosen One, the Christ. According to the writings of the earliest believers (which we call the New Testament), Jesus Christ lived out a life that provides us a complete understanding of what we should be like.

We humans were created to be like the One Who created us. Jesus Christ showed us what our Creator is like. Now we can set our goals, modeled after the life of Jesus, and begin to achieve our fullest potential.

"Is that all there is to it?" you may ask. "Is that all I have to do – to model my life after the life of this one man? If I read His story in the Gospels and list all the distinguishing characteristics of His life, His words and thoughts, then set my goals accordingly, is that all I have to do to achieve my full potential of being like God?"

An early writer answered these questions too: **...to all who received him, to those who believed in his name, he gave the right to become children of God – children born not of natural descent, nor of human decision or a husband's will, but born of God** (John 1:12,13). If we are to be like God, a new creation is necessary.

In the beginning we were created with the potential to be like our Creator. If nothing had happened to the original purpose and order of creation, then nothing more would have been needed than to live according to our natural impulses and desires. That kind of living, in itself, would have led to a godlike life in every person. But something did happen. Something was allowed to come into man and his world to mar the image and likeness of God. The Bible calls it sin: disobedience; failure to trust God, the Creator; refusal to acknowledge the divine control over man's life; a selfish pride that demands its own way, no matter who is hurt; an unnatural desire to control others, to manipulate circumstances for personal advantage and benefit.

All of these things are sin. And sin has robbed us of our original potential. It has corrupted our ability to be like God by living according to our human nature. Because of our corrupted nature, now in order for us to be like God, something more is needed than simply "doing what comes naturally."

We need to be newly created, to be "born again," as Jesus phrased it. (John 3:3.) We need to go through a new creation of our being. This new creation restores us to our original, natural potential and gives us an extra bonus. No longer are we simply created in God's image and likeness, now we are re-created as the very children of God. Once we were among the created beings of God, higher than any other part of creation, with a more noble purpose and greater power. But now, we are more: we are part of the family of God. We are the children of God, and God is our Father.

"Wait a minute," you may say. "Aren't we all God's children? Isn't every human being a child of God, and isn't God the Father of every person?"

The answer is yes and no. Yes, we are all the children of God, in the sense that our life comes from Him. The Apostle Paul recognized this fact, as we read in his speech to the Athenians, in which he said of God:

> "...he himself gives all men life and breath and everything else. From one man he made every nation of men, that they should inhabit the whole earth; and he determined the times set for them and the exact places where they should live. God did this so that men would seek him and perhaps reach out for him and find him, though he is not far from each one of us. 'For in him we live and move and

have our being.' As some of your own poets have
said, 'We are his offspring.'"

Acts 17:25-28

If a parent is one who gives life to another person,
then God, as the Creator, is the Father of us all. He is both
father and mother to us, in the sense that we are the offspring of this single divine being. He "breathed into" us
"the breath of life," and we became living beings. (Gen.
2:7.) God gave us life, and, in that sense, God has fathered
and given birth to every human being.

In our creation, God intended, too, that we should
be to Him as children are to a father. The design was that
each of us would enjoy that intimate parent-child relationship. Adam and Eve walked and talked with God in the
garden in the cool of the day, according to the Genesis
account. This image suggests a very intimate relationship
between human beings and God. When we turn over to
the New Testament, we find that this lost relationship is
exactly what Jesus came to restore (e.g., see Luke 15).

But according to Jesus (in John 3:3), a new birth is
necessary in order to restore that relationship. Our original
creation and the natural life that we share is not enough;
sin has spoiled it. Our pride, our unbelief, our rebellion –
all of these things have separated us human beings from
God so that a new beginning is needed. The New
Testament says that this new beginning must be by faith.
We must put our trust in Jesus Christ and in what He has
done for us. We cannot get rid of our own sin; but Jesus
has done it for us. We cannot conquer our doubt and
unbelief; but Jesus will give us the faith we need. We cannot change our inner life; but Jesus will do it by the Spirit
He places within us. We must be born again, Jesus said;

and when we are, we are ready to start living as the children of our heavenly Father.

What a fantastic goal for life: to live as the children of God. *Set it as your goal in life to achieve the highest potential of your existence: to be like God, your heavenly Father.*

Consider these six ways to achieve that goal:

1. Be living proof that your Father exists.

2. Imitate your Father.

3. Trust your Father to provide what is best for you.

4. Honor your Father.

5. Link the family to future generations.

6. Live for the future.

Your goal for life is to be like your Father in heaven. You are out to achieve that goal. Where do you begin?

The first step is to:

Be Living Proof That Your Father Exists

Other people are not sure that God exists. They have heard rumors that He lives somewhere; but they are not at all sure that those rumors are true. It is up to you and me to prove – to be living proof – that God exists.

Think of the woman who walks up to a boy and looks him over. She glances sideways at him; then she comes closer, scrutinizing every feature. She notes the way he stands, or holds his head, or the way he talks. She says to the boy, "I think I know your father; isn't he...?" By looking at the son, she knows who the father is.

That's the way it should be with us. The way we look, walk, talk, and act, the way we treat other people, the dreams we pursue, the faith we express, the hope and love we share – all of these things make us living proof that our Father exists. Other people look at us; they glance sideways at us; they scrutinize us; and, finally, they say, "Don't I know your Father?"

Steps one and two toward achieving your goal are closely related. Step two is:

Imitate Your Father

The way we become living proof that our Father exists is by imitating Him. Children imitate their parents unconsciously, at first. From the time they are infants, if they are around both their mother and father, children will begin acting, talking, walking, and reacting to other people in the same way their parents do. Only as they grow older do children consciously imitate – or rebel against imitating – their parents.

The key here is the fact that, from infancy, children live in an intimate relationship with their parents. Out of that intimacy, they easily learn to be like the ones who brought them into being.

The key to imitating your Father is having an intimate relationship with Him. Talk with Him. Listen to Him speak. Read the scriptures through which (as we believe) God speaks to us. Have fellowship with the rest of the family (the Church) so they can encourage you and help you to become like the Father. Spend time in prayer and meditation so you can be in direct contact with the Father at all times.

There is another key to this imitation of God, one that seems more practical if you are a little hesitant about developing the intimacy with God which I have just described: *come to know the Father through the One Who came to reveal Him.*

No one has ever seen God. How can anyone know Who He is? How can anyone say, "This is what God is like!"? Yet, one man did. Here is what Jesus of Nazareth (speaking as the Son of God) said about His heavenly Father:

> ..."I tell you the truth, the Son can do nothing by himself; he can do only what he sees his Father doing, because whatever the Father does the Son also does. For the Father loves the Son and shows him all he does...."
>
> **John 5:19,20**

When one of the disciples said, "Lord, show us the Father and that will be enough for us," Jesus responded:

> ..."Don't you know me, Philip, even after I have been among you such a long time? Anyone who has seen me has seen the Father. How can you say, 'Show us the Father'? Don't you believe that I am in the Father, and that the Father is in me? The words I say to you are not just my own. Rather, it is the Father, living in me, who is doing his work. Believe me when I say that I am in the Father and the Father is in me...."
>
> **John 14:9-11**

To know what Jesus is like is to know what God is like. To read in the Gospels about Jesus is to read about God. To discover what Jesus was like – how He lived, what He taught, how He treated people – is to discover what our Father in heaven is like. For Jesus and the Father are one. To know the Son is to know the Father.

Jesus said that to see Him is to see God. That claim is startling. It is unique among the great religious teachers in history. No other person ever made such a claim for Himself. Only Jesus. You can accept that claim, or you can reject it. If you accept it, and begin to live in accordance with it, then you can begin to achieve your goal in life. You can begin, by imitating Jesus, to imitate your Father, and thereby begin to achieve your life goal of becoming like God.

The third step toward achieving the goal of becoming like God is:

Trust Your Father to Provide What Is Best for You

Trust is an essential part of any parent-child relationship. Children must learn to trust their parents to provide whatever they need to be healthy, well-cared for, protected and secure in life. Whatever the needs of their children may be, good parents will do everything in their power to meet those needs. In fact, most parents will do everything they can to provide much more than the mere necessities of life. Most parents will go far beyond provision of basic needs.

If we love our children enough to provide them with everything they need, and much more besides, then surely we can believe that God, our heavenly Father, loves us enough to do the same for His children. Not only will He provide everything we need, but He will give us much of what we want beyond our basic needs. If our desires are good, not too extravagant, not wasteful or selfish or harmful to ourselves or others – if our wants can be satisfied within the limits of His desires for us – then the Father will give us "all these things" as well.[3]

Learn to trust God for all your needs and much of your desires. That trust is vital to your relationship with Him. Most parents do not have the money to satisfy every desire of their children. We want to give good things to our children, but often we simply cannot afford to do so. Because of our limitations, we can't give them everything. But our heavenly Father has all the resources necessary to fully satisfy every desire that is good and appropriate. He has promised to give us what we ask for in faith. Believe that promise. Trust your Father.

The "flip side" of this trust helps us to achieve our goal of becoming like God. Generosity is a divine characteristic. An unselfish desire to give, motivated by love, is a mark of God upon our lives. If we are to be like our heavenly Father, we must learn generosity, unselfish giving.

We learn to trust God to give good things to us; and, in receiving His gifts, we learn the spirit of generosity. We begin to want to share what we have with others. Because we were in need, and God gave to us to meet our needs, so now we give to others to meet their needs. The same trusting spirit which enables us to receive God's gifts will motivate us to give to others the very things we have received. So it is not so much the receiving of God's gifts, but the generous giving of those gifts to others so they can share in our wealth, that makes us truly like our heavenly Father.

---

[3] I realize that this discussion of parents' providing for their children does not fit the experience of many people in our world. Many are caught up in poverty (in an oppressive economic system) which makes it impossible for them to provide even the bare necessities for their children. But that situation, too, becomes the concern of the Church; to seek freedom from these systems for all people so that all can live up to their full potential.

The fourth step toward achieving your goal is:

Honor Your Father

The traditional word for *honor* is "glorify." We are told to glorify our Father Who is in heaven. I chose to use the word *honor* because I think it helps us to more readily understand our responsibility. In fact, if we begin by examining the negative side of this word, it becomes very easy to understand its positive meaning.

Think of it, first, on the human level. If a son curses his father, he dishonors his parent. If that child is disobedient, unruly, even violent toward the family, he dishonors his family. If that child grows up and disowns his parents and family by living as a rebel in society, he dishonors both parents and family.

Think of it in spiritual terms, then. If people are hateful or malicious toward others, using the name of God to support such talk, they dishonor God. If they are disobedient to God's will, consciously refusing to do what they know the scriptures say they should, going against their own consciences, perhaps even being violent and malicious toward other people, they dishonor God and God's family. If people grow into adulthood and disown the Church, refuse to acknowledge God's control over their lives, and live as rebels in society, they dishonor both God and the Church.

To honor our Father, then, is to do the opposite of these negative things. We honor God by speaking gently, humbly, and lovingly, by treating others with kindness, patience, and forbearance. We are forgiving toward them, because God has forgiven us. We find out what God's will is for us, then we determine to do it to the full extent of the power within us. We choose to do what is right, what we know to be good. As we grow from childhood to maturity, we commit ourselves even more to serving God among His people, to building up His kingdom on earth, to making the Church larger and spiritually stronger than it has ever been before. We live under the laws of society as responsible citizens; and we live according to the principles of the Kingdom of God as mature members of His family.

We honor God by honoring His children. We cannot glorify God by what we say at church, and then go out and dishonor people by the way we treat them. If we dishonor other human beings by unkind, selfish, hateful words or actions toward them, we dishonor God. But if we treat others with love, kindness, patience and gentleness, we honor God. The choice is ours.

Step five toward achieving the goal of becoming like God is:

Link the Family to Future Generations

The primary reason for having children has always been to provide for the future of the family and of the human race. Each family is concerned that there will be children, grandchildren, great-grandchildren, and so on into countless future generations. No family wants to die out because there have been no offspring. Most people consider it a tragedy to know that a person is the last remaining member of a long family line. When that person is gone, the family will be forever lost to history.

In the same way, one of our responsibilities as children of the Father is to provide for future generations. It is true that only God gives new life. God alone is the Father (and Mother) Who gives birth to persons in every generation. But it is also true that He has given us the work of spreading the Word by which that life is received. It is the Word of God, preached and taught and shared with all human beings, which gives life to all who will believe. When we share that Word with other people and they believe it, we become directly responsible for the new birth which occurs. In a sense, we become the believer's spiritual parents. We give birth to others through the labor of our love, our prayers, our continuing efforts to bring them to faith.

God wants us to be spiritual parents. When a person whom I have helped to come to faith then helps another person believe, the one who helps has then become a parent, and I have become a grandparent. The process continues through every generation. That is what the Church calls evangelism: sharing the Word of God, the Gospel of Jesus Christ, so that others will believe and have new life. This process of evangelism is the procreative work of the Church. God creates and re-creates; but, in a sense, it is the Church which procreates so that God's family will continue and not be forever lost to history.

One of the ways children look forward to becoming like their parents is in this procreative aspect of life. Most children look forward to the time when they can get married and have children of their own. They eagerly anticipate being able to play a part in carrying the family forward into another generation. That desire to preserve and procreate is a part of living. So we become like our Father when we share in His re-creative work by our procreative work of sharing His Word and helping people come to faith in Jesus Christ, thus receiving the gift of new life.

The sixth, and final, step toward achieving our goal is the decision to:

Live for the Future

The Christian life is firmly rooted in the past. Through the work of Christ – His incarnation, death and resurrection – new life became a possibility for all people. The re-creative work of God began. The Church, the family of God, came into being. This family has continued now for 20 centuries and has a glorious (if somewhat stained) past. It has its traditions and history which we dare not forget. Rather, the family should learn – and learn from – its own history.

In our life as Christians, we must look to the past. We must also live in the present. What we do, what we accomplish for the future, we do in the present. We can never live *in* the future. We cannot sit idly by and wait for some future event to bring about everything we hope for now. We must obey God today; we must serve Him now; we must do in the present what He has commanded us to do now.

But there is hope for the future that is not fulfilled in the present. We should live with anticipation to see the fulfillment of all that God has promised His family. Our assurance that God will give us everything He has promised gives us hope to go on in the face of tragedy, sorrow, grief and tremendous difficulties. Hope enables us to keep believing. The future pulls us forward through our troubles, as a rope might pull us through quicksand to safety.

God has already given us many gifts. We thank Him for them. We live with gratitude for all that He has already done for us. But we live with the confidence that whatever has already been done is but a token, a sample, of what God will do for us in the future. The portion of the divine inheritance which has been given to us is just a foretaste of the vast riches of our full inheritance as the children of God.

People who have rich parents live in anticipation of the time when they will receive their rightful and full inheritance. Many have to wait a long time. But they know that inheritance will one day be theirs. When it finally becomes a reality, in a sense, they become more like their parents than ever before. They now have the confidence that comes with knowing that everything is taken care of for the rest of their life. Their feeling of power and confidence at receiving their full inheritance is nothing compared to the power and confidence that will be ours when, as the children of God, we receive our full inheritance.

Conclusion

Dream bigger and go farther than you ever have before. If your dreams are limited to money, fame or power, they are too small. If your highest goal is anything less than becoming like God, you are limiting yourself and keeping yourself from developing to your fullest potential.

Dare to be more than a person who is *only* human. Dare to be *fully* human – to experience the full potential of your creation through the new creation of Jesus Christ. Dare to become a child of God through faith in Christ.

Do everything you can right now, right where you are, in your own circumstances, to accomplish your goal, to achieve your full potential. Why settle for less than the best? Be like your Father in heaven.

3

Take Charge of Your Life

In this book we are learning how to be leaders and how to train others to become leaders. An important part of leadership preparation is learning to take charge. Taking charge suggests being in control. But what are we to control? Does being a leader mean controlling other people? Does it mean exercising power over the lives of others? Are power and leadership synonymous? Not necessarily. But self-control and leadership are.

If you want to be a leader, you must *exercise control over your own life*. You must take charge of yourself, your feelings, your thoughts – all that you think and say and do. You must know that you are in charge of yourself in all circumstances. Self-control produces self-confidence. Seeing your self-control, others will recognize you as a person who can be trusted and will then be willing to place their confidence in you. Self-control and confidence go together.

I believe that we were created to be in control. I also believe that a lack of control – or a feeling that we have lost control – goes against the natural grain of our being. Both the psalmist and the writer of the Creation story in the Bible agree that we were created to be in control. Consider these verses:

> **When I consider your heavens, the work of your fingers, the moon and the stars, which you have set in place,**

> **What is man that you are mindful of him? the son of man that you care for him?**
>
> **You made him a little lower than the heavenly beings and crowned him with glory and honor.**
>
> **You made him ruler over the works of your hands; you put everything under his feet** (control).
>
> **Psalm 8:3-6**
>
> **Then God said, "Let us make man in our image, in our likeness, and let them rule...over all the earth...."**
>
> **So God created man in his own image, in the image of God he created him; male and female he created them.**
>
> **God blessed them and said to them, "Be fruitful and increase in number; fill the earth and subdue it...."**
>
> **Genesis 1:26-28**

If we were created to be in charge of all of God's creation, and if we are the highest part of that creation, then surely we are to be in control over ourselves first of all.

The New Testament suggests as much. Jesus and the writers of the Early Church agree on this principle. Phrases appear in the ancient writings which set forth our responsibility for ourselves. They say things like, "Let your light shine"; "Put off the old...put on the new"; "Clothe yourselves"; "Be at peace"; "Love one another." All of these phrases (and a great many more) make it plain that we are to be in control of our own lives.

The temptation, of course, is to try to take charge of the lives of other people without controlling our own. Jesus spoke about this situation in these words:

"Why do you look at the speck of sawdust in your brother's eye and pay no attention to the plank in your own eye? How can you say to your brother, 'Let me take the speck out of your eye,' when all the time there is a plank in your own eye? You hypocrite, first take the plank out of your own eye, and then you will see clearly to remove the speck from your brother's eye."

Matthew 7:3-5

And Paul spoke to this issue:

Each one should test his own actions. Then he can take pride in himself, without comparing himself to somebody else, for each one should carry his own load.

Galatians 6:4,5

Many of the New Testament writers had something to say about self-control, temperance, moderation and the necessity of obedience to God's commands. Taking control over our own lives is of primary importance to all who want to be leaders.

How do we begin to take charge? We start by realizing and believing this truth:

God Put Us in Charge

By the action of creation, by the fact of our existence, God put us – along with all other human beings – in charge of His creation. Everything which God has created is under our supervision, under our control. But that control begins with ourselves. We must learn to take charge of ourselves before we can rightfully take charge of anything else.

But we must also understand this truth:

143

God Put Us in Charge as Stewards

We are responsible to God. We are accountable to Him for all that we do with what He has given us. We are not owners; we are only caretakers. Whether we speak of the earth itself – or of our possessions, bodies, or minds – we are only caretakers and stewards, not owners. We are accountable to God for what we do with the bodies and minds (as well as with the rest of creation) which He has entrusted to us. But this fact does not in any way lessen our responsibility to be in charge.

Dare to think that you are in charge of this world. Dream big; think big, act big – in the sense of believing that God has given you control over things that you have always felt controlled you. Most people feel that they have no control over the circumstances of their lives. They live each day with the constant fear of what might happen to them. The reason they live in fear is because they have lost faith in their power to control the forces that seem to affect their lives.

You may say, "But I don't have any control over what other people do; I can't *make* them do what I think they should." Of course, that's true. God has given each of us the freedom to choose how we will act, how we will live our lives. Even God does not override that freedom of choice, under most circumstances. So, of course, we can't pretend that we have any power over other people's wills and lives. We can't make others bend to our will. As long as we live, people will constantly do things that will have a negative impact on our lives – if we allow it to do so. That is the key: our lives will be negatively affected by the actions of others – *if we allow it*.

Being in control over our own lives means refusing to allow the negative circumstances of our outward lives to control our inner selves. How we respond and react to other people and their attitudes and actions, how we respond to the circumstances surrounding us, is our choice. We may not always be able to control the circumstances; we cannot control other people and what they choose to think and say and do, but *we can always control our own feelings and how we choose to respond to what is happening.* That inner control of our own being is an important responsibility – and a vital factor – in becoming a leader.

Consider this simple diagram:

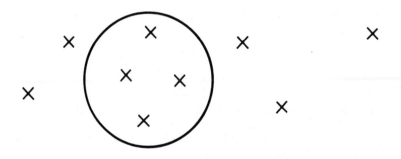

The circle represents each individual life. What is inside the circle is within our control. It is our responsibility. Whether it is fear, anger, hatred, and malice, or hope, forgiveness, love and gentleness, it is our responsibility and choice. We can choose. We can control it.

What is outside the circle – the circumstances of our lives – is often out of our control: earthquakes, war, famine, sickness, personal tragedy or the way others treat us. We usually cannot control these things. But we can control how we react or respond to them. The control of our inner selves is always our responsibility, whether or not we can control our outward circumstances.

How do we maintain control over our own lives? If we do not control the circumstances of our lives (and very often we do not), how can we hope to be in charge of the rest of the world? If we cannot control how other people treat us, or even control their relationship to us, how can we say that we are in charge?

Here are a few examples:

* Your boss criticizes you for doing a poor job when you have done the best you know how. What is your reaction? Do you get defensive and start making excuses, recounting all the reasons why it wasn't your fault that the results were not satisfactory? Do you snap back, and probably get fired? Or do you honestly and sincerely say, "I'm sorry my work didn't meet your standards. I'll do my best to do better next time"? If you choose this last option, your choice suggests that you are in charge of yourself.

* As you and your husband are getting ready for work, he notices some household chore that didn't get done the evening before. He begins to complain about how you never get your housework done now that you are working outside the home. Do you argue back that if he made enough money you wouldn't have to work? Do you snap back and point out how the yard and garage aren't quite what they should be either? Do you sulk for the rest of the day and take it out on him that night by neglecting or ignoring him? Or do you patiently remind him that it was a joint decision for you to go to work; do you gently (but firmly) suggest that since both of you

sleep, eat, and live in the home, perhaps there are some
things he might help you with around the house? This last
choice reveals a woman with self-control.

* You are a high school or college student. Your
teacher notices something you failed to do early in the
term. Now he reminds you of it in front of the class every
time you fall short of perfection. In addition, he grades off
on some papers that you know are good. In essence, he
treats you unfairly just because of one past mistake. What
do you do? Do you let the situation go, hoping he will
change his attitude and actions toward you? Do you
decide to just take your chances on getting a good grade at
the end of term? Do you get back at the teacher by goofing
off in class and doing only the bare minimum on your
school work? Do you complain to your parents about the
teacher, telling them enough of the story to motivate them
to make an issue of the situation? Or do you go privately
to the teacher and explain to him politely and respectfully
what you think is happening, asking him to give you a
fresh start, promising to do your best work for the rest of
the term? This last choice shows self-control – it indicates a
person who is in charge.

* You are 80 years old and have developed several
health problems, all of them common to old age. You don't
feel good very often; in fact, much of the time you feel rot-
ten. You have a small apartment where you could shut
yourself away and never have to get out, except for an
occasional trip to the store or to church. Even though it
gets lonely at times, self-isolation appeals to you. But your
friends and family have started complaining that you have
shut them out of your life. What do you decide to do
about the situation? How do you respond to the concern

of those who care the most about you? Do you do what is most pleasing to you, regardless of how it affects others? Do you force yourself to get out and circulate, even though it makes you tired and miserable? Or do you look for a possible alternative: do you consult with your doctor and work out a sensible diet and exercise program which will allow you to meet your obligations to others and still have time and energy to do the things that you enjoy? Choosing this last option reveals a person who is in full charge of his or her own life – however long (or short) it may be.

* * * * * * * *

God put you (along with the rest of us) in charge of all of His creation. We are the highest part of that creation, and God has put us in charge of ourselves. We are in control – accountable to God alone, ultimately. In one way or another, each of us is accountable to other people: spouse, parents, teachers, children, employer, landlord, government. But in the final analysis, we are responsible only to God for what we do with our lives.

We need to stop allowing other people to dictate to us what we are to do and how we should react to them. We must let God tell us how to live. He will tell us to obey our parents, respect our boss, love our neighbor, care for the sick, listen to the wise and provide for the needy. But even when we have done these things, we have never relinquished the control of ourselves. We have maintained self-discipline, self-control, patience, joy and a forgiving spirit. What do these things have to do with taking charge?

We let people control our lives when we grow bitter toward them because of their injustice or abuse or selfishness toward us. When we refuse to forgive them, they control our emotions and our reactions by their past deeds. Our growing resentment and bitterness dominate our thinking and control our actions. They even cause disease in our bodies – all because of what some other person has done to us.

We must never allow other people to control us.

We let people control our lives when their stupid and insensitive words and actions cause us to become angry and impatient. How other people act is their responsibility. But whether we react in love and kindness rather than in anger and impatience is our choice.

If you would like to be a leader, make the choice to live in love, kindness, patience and gentleness. Choose to control your emotions, your thoughts, your words, your actions. Be molded by the positive virtues of life. Take charge of yourself.

To take charge of our lives does not mean to control others. It simply means that we refuse to allow others to control us in a negative way. We should never think that "taking dominion over the earth" means taking control over others. We were not created to be masters, but servants. We were meant to serve God and other people, not to rule over anyone. Each of us is responsible for our own life, individually; we are not to control or to be controlled, except by God. We are all in charge, together, each one responsible for his or her individual part.

Consider five areas of living which we are to be in charge of:

Family

Whether, in your present situation, you are a parent, child, grandparent, uncle or aunt, you have your part to play in the family unit. If you are a child under 18 years of age, your part is to honor and obey your parents. If you are a parent with children at home, your part is to bring them up in "the nurture and admonition of the Lord," to teach them how to live in this world as mature, responsible adults. If you are a grandparent, or an uncle or aunt, you are in a supportive role. It is your part to help parents and children work together to achieve and maintain a positive, loving home life. If you are married, you are to love, honor, cherish, respect, serve and be faithful to your spouse through all the years of your shared life. You are to support and strengthen your spouse, encouraging him or her to be that way toward you. Whatever your role, accept your part; take charge of yourself in the family relationship.

Church

If you believe in Jesus Christ as Lord and Savior, you are part of the Church, a member of the Body. Your responsibilities will differ from those of other members of the Body – as the functions of arms differ from those of legs – but each of us has one goal: to help the Body to function efficiently and effectively, keeping it healthy and whole, nurturing and strengthening it to do its proper work. Be in control of your part; don't worry about someone else's responsibility; carry out your own duties and help make the Church a healthy, functioning body.

Work

Only one person can be president of the company or chairman of the board. Only one person in each organization can be the chief executive officer. Only a few others can hold supervisory positions. Most people must, by the very nature of things, do their work under the supervision of others. But each person must do the work assigned to him or her. Each of us must fulfill our individual task, for that is our responsibility. That is what we are in charge of.

The privileges that go with being a CEO, for instance, require much more responsibility than most people are able or willing to accept. Don't envy someone else his job or position. Accept your work; do it to the best of your ability; do it with a willing spirit and a cheerful attitude. (More about this subject in Chapter 6.)

Society

Whether you and I like it or not, we are part of a certain society. We don't always approve of how our government operates or how other people in our community live. We don't like how some people dress, talk or act. But we are part of the society in which we live. If we refuse to accept responsibility as part of that society, if we turn our backs on other people, if we neglect our rights and duties as citizens of our society, we turn over to others control of this part of our lives.

If we educate our children in schools which are segregated by race or religion, if we refuse to participate in activities supported by the rest of the community, if we do not vote, if we turn the arts (music, literature, architecture, painting, sculpture, theater) over to those who do not believe, we relinquish the control of our world to those who do not recognize the authority of its divine Creator. If we do these things, then we fail God.

As Christians, we must take responsibility for our part in the proper functioning and operation of this world.

Do your part in the society in which you live. Help to make the world a better place to live – for everyone. Be accountable to God and serve the needs of those around you.

Nature

Ecology is everyone's concern. Pollution is everybody's business. The threat of catastrophic destruction due to widespread abuse of the earth or nuclear devastation is your responsibility and mine. The resources of this planet we live on are rapidly decreasing due to population growth, neglect, abuse and exploitation. The size of the planet is also shrinking due to instant communication that informs us of everything that takes place, virtually as soon as it happens. The stability of the planet is more and more put in jeopardy as nations and peoples vie for control of vital, diminishing land and raw material resources. All of these factors must become the concern of responsible Christians.

If the human race is to survive, personal and national interests must be sacrificed for the sake of interpersonal and international interests. This sacrifice will require leadership. The Church must have a part in that leadership. Those who want to lead must be prepared to be leaders in the world as well as in the Church and in Christian homes.

Christian homes and the churches have been weakened by what is happening in the world around us. We can no longer ignore it, hoping it will go away or be resolved by someone else. We have been put in charge of this world. We are responsible and accountable to God for what happens to His creation. The responsibility that begins within us must be expanded until we, as leaders, take charge even in the fight against pollution, for instance.

Conclusion

In our churches, we have preached *against* things. We have preached against immorality, corruption in government, drug abuse – against almost everything that we can be against. It is time that we started preaching *for* things. It is time we began to let the world know what we are *for*, what we think *should* happen, how we think these problems *can* be solved. I don't mean the preaching done from the pulpits. We need that, too. But we need to preach, to proclaim, in all of our words and actions and influence, that we are responsible to God for what we do with our lives – whether in the family, in the church, at work, in society or in the natural world.

We have placed a great deal of blame for our problems without offering any solutions. We must stop laying blame. Instead, we must start solving problems. Blaming others is one way to avoid taking control. Shifting the blame to other people is how we excuse ourselves from taking charge and becoming effective leaders.

Start now. Begin today. Be positive. Look for solutions. Be in control. Take charge. Be a leader.

4

Live the Good Life

When we talk of achieving our potential, most people think of becoming successful. When they think of success, they think of money, career and fame, or of houses, land, cars and clothes. What about you? What *is* the good life to you? When you think about living the good life, what do you associate with that life? Make a list. Then read on.

Now that you have your list of things that you consider to be part of the good life, let me rephrase the question: what is good about life? Make another list. It will be somewhat different, no doubt. Perhaps your list will include such things as friends, love, accomplishments, helping others. Aren't these the things that make life good for us? Make your own list. Compare it to the first one. Then read on.[1]

The good life can be defined in many ways. Let me turn the words around and make this brief, basic statement: life, in itself, is good. Life is good; and if what you are living now is not good, it is not life as it was meant to be lived. When God created all things, including human beings, He looked over all His creation and said, "It is very good."

---

[1] Many people in our world think that life is *not* good. To them the good life would be one good meal a day and a roof over their head. But the good life, as I define it here, is available to every person, regardless of economic or political circumstances.

Life – as God created and intended it for us – is good.

Now, let me turn these words around once more and expand them a little: life is to be lived in such a way that it can be called good. As God intended it, the good life has very little to do with how much money we make, what kind of job we hold, how well known we are, or any other such circumstance of life.

The good life is life that is lived in such a way that it can be called good.

What this statement means to us is the subject of the rest of this chapter.

One scripture passage, Titus 2:11-15, provides us a basis for describing this good life. From what this passage suggests, we can say that in living the good life, we look first to the past, then to the present, and only then to the future. Here is the passage:

> For the grace of God that brings salvation has appeared to all men. It teaches us to say "No" to ungodliness and worldly passions, and to live self-controlled, upright and godly lives in this present age, while we wait for the blessed hope – the glorious appearing of our great God and Savior, Jesus Christ, who gave himself for us to redeem us from all wickedness and to purify for himself a people that are his very own, eager to do what is good.
>
> These, then, are the things you should teach. Encourage and rebuke with all authority. Do not let anyone despise you.

In Living the Good Life, We Look to the Past

We look back to Jesus Christ. Our life is possible through what He has done for us. Our life is from Him.

Without Him there is no life. *Christ is the source and foundation for the good life.* This passage says two things about Christ which are important for us to understand.

First, **...the grace of God that brings salvation** (which) **has appeared to all men** (v. 11) has appeared to us through Jesus Christ. God's grace is known to us, and given to us, through Christ. It can be understood (if it can be understood at all) only by looking to Christ. He has appeared to show us the good life and to make it available to all. He lived a good life; no one denies that He was a good man. His teachings are good; nearly everyone agrees that His words and sermons are good for all people to live by. If we follow His example, our lives will follow a good path. If we are like Him in what we do and say, we will be good persons. That truth, too, is almost universally accepted.

The Christian message goes a step farther. When Jesus died and rose again, He conquered the power of sin and paid the price for sin so that all human beings might be free from its grip. When we are freed from the power and penalty of our sin, we enter a new life that is good. We enter the New Creation; we become new persons. We receive a new nature that is now righteous and good in its inner being. Now that we have once again been created good by God through Christ, we are freed and enabled to live the good life – a life that is good – as we follow the teachings and example of Jesus Christ[2]

The second thing this passage says about Christ is that He died to redeem and purify us. We are to look back

[2] Receiving this new life does not mean that we are made sinless. But we now have a power available to us that will enable us to do what is right, if we choose to do it.

to Him **...who gave himself for us to redeem us from all wickedness and to purify for himself a people that are his very own, eager to do what is good** (v. 14). There is more to the meaning of these two words than meets the eye, but the core significance of our redemption and purification is that Christ died to take away all that is *bad* and bring us into all that is *good*.

The good life (a life that is lived in such a way that it can be called good) *can be lived fully only through Jesus Christ*.

Because only Jesus Christ died to redeem and purify us, only His death makes possible this vital transformation of our being to enable us to live a life that is truly good. Before Calvary, it was impossible; now it is possible, in Christ.

In Living the Good Life, We Look to the Present

This passage suggests that God's grace, and the life that is now ours in Christ, teaches us when to say "no" and when to say "yes." One major problem in living is our ambivalence. We can't make decisions. We don't know when to say "no" to something and when to say "yes." Too often, we say "no" or "yes" to the wrong things. We are confused by the constant pressures of our peers – and the media and commericals and a hundred other forces – to the point that we can't discern between the negative and the positive, the bad and the good. But God's grace in Christ teaches us this discernment.

We learn to say "no" to anything that dishonors either God or His creation (to ungodliness and worldly passions):

* If we ingest or inhale something harmful to our bodies, which God has created, we dishonor them.

* If we join ourselves to another person in sexual intercourse without a full commitment of our lives and ourselves in marriage, we dishonor that person, ourselves and God.

* If we treat other people in a malicious, resentful, angry, jealous or exploitive way, we dishonor God and His creation.

* If we misuse, abuse, or waste anything God has given us, we dishonor it and Him.

* If we spend our time or money or energies entirely for our own selfish gratifications, without any thought for God or other people, we dishonor the whole spectrum of life.

When we learn to say "no" to all these things, and refuse to dishonor God and His creation, including ourselves, in any way, we have taken the first step toward the good life. We take the second step when we say "yes."

We say "yes" to self-control. We learn to control our bodies, our words, our minds, our time and our money in such a way that we honor God and serve others. In that way, we honor ourselves and grow in our self-esteem. We learn to *say "yes" to goodness.* Goodness is simply the quality of life that is good, that is consistent with the nature of God, that is lived in a way that will honor God and all that He has created. Goodness is the opposite of the things mentioned in the previous section:

* Goodness is putting into and onto our bodies only those things that honor them and their Creator.

* Goodness is joining ourselves to another person only in full commitment in a marriage relationship.

* Goodness is treating others with love, kindness, gentleness, humility, compassion and justice.

* Goodness is using our time, energy and possessions in ways that will serve others, honor God and prove our self-respect.

We also learn to *say "yes" to spirituality.* In other words, we simply learn to focus our thoughts on God. When we center our lives on God – His love, righteousness, justice, mercy, compassion, power and all else that belongs to Him – we learn to pray, to listen to the Word of God, to cultivate fellowship with other believers, to discipline ourselves in the spiritual areas of the good life.

In Living the Good Life, We Look to the Future

We look to the perfect life that is ahead of us. There will come a time when all good things will be completed. All that God has promised to those who love Him will be given to them. The New Testament says that day will come at **...the glorious appearing of our great God and Savior, Jesus Christ...**(Titus 2:13). There are many and varied ideas of how this great event will take place, but that it will happen remains an undisputed truth for all believers in Christ. It is that event, that day, that appearing, toward which we look. We anticipate it with hope. We look for it to come with great longing, knowing that all good things will be fulfilled and will reach their completion at that time.

We can be satisfied with nothing less than the continual pursuit of the goal of perfection. We can never be idle in this life, convinced that we have somehow arrived at the ultimate state of perfection – not until that day of perfection has come. So *we must always, daily, be working toward the achievement of that goal of perfect life, perfect goodness.* Anything short of that perfection cannot satisfy us. It will never be enough. But we also know that we can never achieve total perfection until Christ comes again. It will never be a reality for us until then. So we press on; we keep moving ahead; we keep striving toward that goal, always working to achieve our fullest potential of perfection.

The final verse of our passage in Titus is important to note. These things we have been discussing must be at the foundation of what we teach: **These, then, are the things you should teach...**(v. 15), says Paul.

In our churches, we are to teach people how to live the good life. We are to teach them to look to Christ, Who has given us life and Who died to redeem and purify us. We are to teach people to live in the present, learning to say "no" and "yes" at the proper time to the appropriate parts of living. We are to teach them to look forward to the time when Christ will appear, always pressing on today toward the goal of perfection that will be ours that day.

The good life is what the Church should teach. It is what we should have, how we should live. The good life is yours for the living. Live it to the fullest.

5

Make the Right Choice

Many people talk about how we should be fully human; and they link that concept to our right of choice and decision-making. They say that we can choose to become all that we were meant to be. I agree. That truth is at the heart of the scriptures. That potential is at the core of Creation.

Some people, when they have done something they know is wrong, say: "Well, after all, I am *only* human." That phrase has been used to excuse and rationalize away every kind of negative habit and undisciplined drive imaginable. Throughout history these words have been the false comfort of people who have chosen to live short of their created potential. The opposite phrase – "I am *fully* human" – leads to a positive, disciplined way of life. When we say, "I am *fully* human," we stop excusing ourselves and rationalizing away our wrong behavior and our failure to live up to our full, God-given potential.

The story of creation shows us what we ought to be. One central fact of our creation is God's gift of the freedom of choice. God put Adam in the garden and gave him freedom to choose to eat of any tree there, except one. Adam had only one limitation placed upon him. He had almost total freedom; he lost that freedom when he knowingly chose the one thing that was denied to him. This act of conscious disobedience is sin.

You and I have been given the same freedom to enjoy the many pleasures of God's creation, the abundance of the life given to us. Not much is denied us. But when we abuse our freedom by choosing that small part of creation that is off limits to us, we lose our freedom, just as Adam did.

Imagine a huge open space filled with light and beauty. Around the edge of that space is emptiness. We have the freedom to roam the entire area of that space of light and beauty. We can enjoy the many delights of it. We could live in the vast open area forever and never exhaust the abundance of its pleasures. But the moment we betray the trust of the One Who placed us there, once we step off into the dark void around the edge, we are lost to the light and must wander aimlessly in the darkness forever. We are trapped by it; we are caught in its grip for eternity. The power of that darkness is too great for us; we can never step back out of it. There is only one possibility of regaining our former place of light and beauty. Only if the One Who put us there in the first place reaches out into the darkness and brings us back – only then can we return to freedom and true enjoyment of life.

If you can imagine what I have just described, you can understand what the Bible says about life and death, heaven and hell, salvation and condemnation, freedom and bondage, righteousness and sin. The open space of light and beauty is the life we were created to live. This life is what we were created to share and enjoy forever. But when we choose to step off into the darkness, we become lost, trapped, enslaved by the unseen powers that lurk there. Nothing we can do is sufficient to enable us to return. Only when God reaches out to bring us back can we return to the freedom, the joy and the beautiful life for which we were created.

The good news (the Gospel) is that, through Jesus Christ, God has already reached out to save, deliver and restore. Even now He is constantly reaching out into the darkness to bring us back to the light. If you will let Him grip you, hold you, and bring you back, then life, in all the fullness of its potential, will be yours.

Once you have allowed the hand of God to bring you back into Life, you are again able to enjoy and share in the freedom of choice that was ours to begin with. Everything that is in the open area is ours to enjoy. We are free to choose – to experience – all that we see within the limits of that space. The limits are defined for us in the pages of the scriptures.

In the sixth chapter of Romans, the Apostle Paul speaks of our freedom in Christ. He tells us that we are free from the grip of that darkness, from the power of sin. We are again free to choose. Verses 5 through 14 provide us the basis for at least three affirmations we can make about our freedom.

AFFIRMATION 1: I am free from sin's power.

> **If we have been united with him in his death, we will certainly also be united with him in his resurrection. For we know that our old self was crucified with him so that the body of sin might be rendered powerless, that we should no longer be slaves to sin – because anyone who has died has been freed from sin.**
>
> **Romans 6:5-7**

I am free from sin's power. I am free to choose to do what is right. I am no longer held in the grip of the power of sin. I am not under the control of my own selfish desires, my evil impulses. I am not under the domination of any power or person except God. I am free.[1]

Can you say those words and mean them? Do you believe that they are true for you? If you can say them, you can begin to experience the freedom for which you were created. If you can say them, even though you don't feel that they are yet true for you, the freedom can be yours. Faith is the inner confirmation that what we cannot yet see is nonetheless real. Put your faith to work. Make these affirmations. Experience your freedom in Christ.

AFFIRMATION 2: I will live for God.

> **Now if we died with Christ, we believe that we will also live with him. For we know that since Christ was raised from the dead, he cannot die again; death no longer has mastery over him. The death he died, he died to sin once for all; but the life he lives, he lives to God.**
>
> **Romans 6:8-10**

I will live for God. I can choose to stop living for myself alone. I can choose to stop living for others who put wrong or unfair pressures on me. I can choose to stop living according to the pressures of my peers or any other source which does not come from faith or true life.

---

[1] Some would say that we are not free from the sinful nature, even though we are new creatures in Christ. They base their idea on the spiritual battle described in Romans 7:14-25. But I believe that Christ *has* rescued us (vv. 24,25) and that we are no longer "slaves to sin." (v. 14.) We are no longer controlled by the sinful nature. (Rom. 7:18,20; 8:5-9; Gal. 5:13-25.) We *are* free to choose to do what is right.

No one who is not motivated by faith will rule over my life. No one who is not of Christ will dominate me. I can now choose for myself what is right, what is of faith, what is true, what is compatible with Christ. I can choose to live for God.

AFFIRMATION 3: I refuse to allow my body to be controlled by wrong desires; I will use my body for things that are pleasing to God.

> In the same way, count yourselves dead to sin but alive to God in Christ Jesus. Therefore do not let sin reign in your mortal body so that you obey its evil desires. Do not offer the parts of your body to sin, as instruments of wickedness, but rather offer yourselves to God, as those who have been brought from death to life; and offer the parts of your body to him as instruments of righteousness. For sin shall not be your master, because you are not under law, but under grace.
>
> **Romans 6:11-14**

I can choose what I will do with my body. It is created by God for good, honorable and beautiful things. I will not dishonor God my Creator, nor myself, nor others, by using my body for dishonorable things. I refuse to allow my body to be controlled by wrong desires. I have the right and freedom to refuse sin. I am stronger than my desires. No one else can tell me what I should want, what kind of desires I should have. I will decide these things for myself under the guidance of Christ Who has given me this freedom. Now only He will be the motivation for what I do with my body.

I will use my body for things that are pleasing to God. He is pleased with beauty, with gentleness. He is pleased with those who live to serve others and who use their bodies in ways that will benefit other people. He is pleased with those who use their bodies in honorable, esteem-building, compassionate ways. I choose to use my body for these things.

Conclusion

The choice is yours. Make the right one. God has once again given you the freedom you had when you were created; in Christ, you have been re-created with the freedom to choose what is good. You do not have to live any longer under the power of sin, in the grip of darkness. You have been brought back into the light. You have been set free. You can live in freedom. You are no longer a slave to sin; now you can be its master.

Make these affirmations:

I AM FREE FROM SIN'S POWER.

I WILL LIVE FOR GOD.

I WILL USE MY BODY FOR THINGS THAT ARE PLEASING TO GOD.

Turn your experience into this reality. Be free. It's your choice.

6

Enjoy Your Work

Work is not something to be avoided or endured; work is to be enjoyed. It is a major part of our lives, in one form or another. The only way to totally avoid it is for other people to take care of us, provide for our needs, clean up after us, do everything for us. Without work, we cannot learn, provide for our families or live in comfortable, clean surroundings. Work is necessary for life. It is also designed to be an enjoyable part of that life. Along with everything that God created for us, our labor is for our enjoyment.

When God created Adam, according to the book of Genesis, He placed him in the garden to work it, to till the ground from which he himself had been formed. Man was created, in part, to work – to take care of the creation which God had put him in charge of. But his work was intended to be a thing of pleasure, surrounded by beauty and delightful things and with a goal of accomplishing something important – the continual, careful cultivation of what God had made.

If we accept the central thesis of this section – that what God created us for is our potential, that which we can achieve – then work becomes part of the purpose of our creation. And enjoyment of our work is seen as part of our potential.

What kind of work? Are we supposed to enjoy every single moment on the job, no matter what we do?

I'm not suggesting exactly that. Let me rephrase and expand my idea: *we can learn to enjoy life while doing any kind of work.* And we can decide to enjoy almost any kind of work we do, at least for a time.

I have worked at a lot of jobs besides that of pastor. I have worked as an upholsterer's apprentice, doing the cleanup and odd jobs that no one else in the shop wanted to do. I have worked in a cheese factory. Part of my job there was to climb inside a huge milk storage tank and mop it out. Many times I slid down the slippery sides and banged my head on the walls.

I once worked as a general laborer in a munitions factory, doing all the dirty, stinking jobs no one wanted to do. At that job, I spent months doing one thing. The factory's inventory included hundreds of barrels of BBs used in making bomb shells. One time there was a fire in the factory, and all the barrels became filled with soot and smoke. So the BBs had to be cleaned. For eight hours a day, day after day, week after week, I dipped out an inch of BBs and poured them into the bottom of a pail which was covered with a screen. Then I had to swish the BBs around in a cleaning solution before dumping them into another clean barrel. This routine was repeated hundreds of times a day, every day, for weeks.

While I was doing that job, one day at lunch another young man about my age came to me and asked why I was always happy and smiling. I certainly didn't think I was always happy and constantly smiling, but obviously something on the inside of me had been showing on the outside. Without even being aware of it, I had been able to enjoy life, even to enjoy my routine, boring work – so much so that others could see my happiness and enjoyment on my face.

I have worked out in the open during the bitter winter months, loading new camper shells onto trucks to be shipped to some warm spot in the nation. I worked for five years in the composing rooms of daily newspapers as a printer, painstakingly putting together page after page of news for other people to skim through and throw away, sometimes without even having read it at all. I worked as a telephone salesman, calling people to try to persuade them to buy something when it was obvious that they didn't even want to talk to me, much less buy from me.

I have done all kinds of work. And in every situation, I have worked hard to do what I am suggesting that you do. It can be done. You can learn to enjoy your work, no matter what kind of work it is.

What kind of work do you do? Do you work for yourself or for someone else? For a large company or a small business? Do you work as a student? That, too, is work to be enjoyed. Do you work as a homemaker, providing comfortable, enjoyable surroundings for your family, seeing that their needs (and yours) are met? Are you a secretary, a janitor, a crew foreman, a salesman, a lawyer, a production-line supervisor, a doctor, a corporation president? Whatever kind of work you do, you can enjoy it.

Two scripture passages provide us a basis for six affirmations that will help us learn to enjoy our work. Read these scriptures. Learn the affirmations; repeat them; determine to live up to them. Then go out and do it. You *can* enjoy your work.

> Then I realized that it is good and proper for a man to eat and drink, and to find satisfaction in his toilsome labor under the sun during the few days of life God has given him – for this is his lot. Moreover, when God gives any man wealth and possessions, and enables him to enjoy them, to accept his lot and be happy in his work – this is a gift of God. He seldom reflects on the days of his life, because God keeps him occupied with gladness of heart.
>
> Ecclesiastes 5:18-20

AFFIRMATION 1: I can enjoy my work.

The book of Ecclesiastes has been neglected in the Church because we have focused so much on the life to come that we have neglected the truth that this life, too, is to be enjoyed. Enjoyment of life is what Ecclesiastes is all about.[2]

"I realized that it is good for a man to eat and drink and find pleasure in his work," concluded the writer. When you realize and accept this basic truth, you can begin to enjoy your work.

As long as we are convinced that work is something to be endured (because we aren't rich enough to get out of it), we will never find any satisfaction in what we do. But when we realize that work is meant to be a part of our potential in living – something to be done with pleasure, something in which we can feel a real sense of accomplish-

---

[2] The writer of this book was pessimistic about human life. He concluded that all the things we spend our lives trying to attain (wealth, knowledge, pleasure) are meaningless. But he did seem to recognize the value of finding pleasure in the simple things of life: work, family, and daily living. (See also Eccl. 2:24-26a; 3:12,13; 7:14a; 8:15; 9:9,10; 11:8a,9; 12:13.)

ment, something that is a *good* (as well as a necessary) part of our lives – then we can begin to enjoy it.

Work was created for us; we were not created for it. The rest of creation was made for our pleasure and enjoyment, not we for it. In 1 Timothy, the Apostle Paul states this fact twice:

> **For everything God created is good, and nothing is to be rejected if it is received with thanksgiving.**
>
> **1 Timothy 4:4**

> **...God...richly provides us with everything for our enjoyment.**
>
> **1 Timothy 6:17**

Our work is to be included in the list of things which God has created and provided for us. It is for our enjoyment. We are not to reject it, but to receive it with thanksgiving. We are to do it with a grateful heart, thankful that we have work to do and that we have the mind and health to be able to do it. Many people don't have these things. They wish they did. We should be thankful for the work God has given us to do.

When we realize and accept this truth – that work was intended for our enjoyment and pleasure – then we can begin to say these words with real conviction. Enjoying our work becomes at least a possibility for us. We know we should enjoy it. We believe we can. So we retrain our minds to tell ourselves that we do. We say with our mouths what we know to be the truth (even if we don't "feel" it inside): "I can enjoy my work."

AFFIRMATION 2: I will be at peace within myself at work.

Ecclesiastes says that when the Lord enables us to enjoy what we have and to be happy in our work, it is a gift from God. Inner peace, in any circumstance, is a gift from the Creator of life. To be happy, content, and at peace within ourselves is a wonderful gift to be received and enjoyed.

Imagine that God is standing in front of you right now, stretching out His hands toward you. In His palm is a gift, beautifully wrapped, with your name on it. You reach out and take it from Him, unwrap it, and open it up. There before you is one of the best gifts you could ever hope to receive – inner peace. Take it; it's yours. Don't refuse it. Don't set it on a shelf and never enjoy it. Inner peace – peace of mind and heart that yields contentment and satisfaction – is yours as a gift. No cost. You can't buy it. You can only receive it and enjoy it forever.

Why not accept that gift? Why continuously make yourself unhappy by refusing to enjoy your work? Why go to work every day wishing you could be someplace else doing something entirely different? Why start each new week thinking how nice it would be not to have to work at all? Why not realize that work is to be enjoyed, that God can give you the peace to enjoy it? Accept that gift, and start a new way of living.

AFFIRMATION 3: I will live each day to the fullest.

The person described in the passage from Ecclesiastes "seldom reflects on the days of his life, because God keeps him occupied with gladness of heart." I suggest that these words can mean that we should not count the days of our earthly labor. Don't count the days until Friday when you can get away from your job "for two whole days." Don't begin your work week on Monday morning wishing it were quitting time on Friday afternoon. Don't count the weeks until your next vacation, marking the days off the calendar, just living for the day you can take off again. Don't do as some people who start in at age 60, or 50, or even 40, counting the years until their retirement.

"Just a few more years," some say, "and I'll be free; I won't have to come to this old job any more."

What a way to live. What a way to die slowly, to wither away, to rot. That way is not life; it's only some kind of existence. It's not being fully human, and it's certainly not enjoyable.

Don't adopt that kind of negative attitude and outlook. Instead, let God keep you occupied with gladness of heart. Let Him be the center and object of your thoughts. Let His dreams for your life fill your mind. Let His peace fill your whole being. Let God's words and promises motivate you to live your life to its fullest potential.

While you are on the job, instead of doing only what you have to, look around and find more work to do. When you have finished that work, ask what else needs to be done. Think for yourself; make yourself useful. Ask for permission to do something that's been neglected but which you know you can do well. Come in a little earlier or stay a little later. Do the best job you can throughout the whole day, every day. Come to work with a sense of excitement about what you can find to do today, about what opportunities the day's work will bring, about what new challenges will surface. Don't count the days; count the accomplishments. Don't look at the negative; focus on the positive. Don't see what's wrong; find out what's right – and enjoy it.

However, there *are* dead-end jobs. There are jobs that will never lead anywhere, jobs in which there is no opportunity for advancement, no new experiences to enjoy, no room for promotion or growth or salary increase, no challenge, no pleasure. If you stay in such a job very long, you will begin to wither and fade away. If you find yourself stuck in a dead-end job, do something about it. Go back to high school or college and get more education. Enroll in night classes at a vocational or technical school to become better trained in what you enjoy doing. If you have sufficient education and training, then ask for a transfer to another job that offers more excitement, opportunity and responsibility. Or just do such fantastic work that your superior will notice you and promote you into such a position.

If your job will never offer anything different or better, then change jobs.[1]

But don't be foolish. Don't quit your job today with no other prospects in view. Start looking, planning and preparing for something better, but hold on to what you have now until that new job materializes. Learn to enjoy life while you perform your present work. You may never enjoy that particular job itself, but you can enjoy living while you work at it. That's the key to happiness in your work: *live each day to its fullest potential, doing your very best at whatever your hand finds to do.*

---

[1] I realize that changing jobs is not always a possibility for everyone. But most people *could* do something about their situation, if they would. Once again, the Church has a responsibility to work toward freeing people from oppressive economic and social situations so they, too, can have an opportunity to realize their fullest potential.

> **Slaves, obey your earthly masters with respect and fear, and with sincerity of heart, just as you would obey Christ. Obey them not only to win their favor when their eye is on you, but like slaves of Christ, doing the will of God from your heart. Serve wholeheartedly, as if you were serving the Lord, not men, because you know that the Lord will reward everyone for whatever good he does, whether he is slave or free.**
>
> **And masters, treat your slaves in the same way. Do not threaten them, since you know that he who is both their Master and yours is in heaven, and there is no favoritism with him.**
>
> **Ephesians 6:5-9**

Our cultural and social circumstances have obviously changed since these words were written. There are no longer slaves and masters, as such, in most of the world. Because of economic injustices, however, the situation for some people is almost that of slavery. And, of course, some people do find themselves in work situations which seem to them almost as hopeless and oppressive as involuntary servitude.

However, the principles of this passage, which govern the relationship of employer and employee, are still applicable to our situation today. So, on the basis of this passage, I would like to suggest three additional affirmations which, I believe, will help us learn to enjoy our work.

AFFIRMATION 4: I will respect my co-workers.

This whole passage suggests that a mutual respect is called for among those who claim to belong to Christ. Obviously, it would be best if all parties involved were committed to the same principle of mutual respect. It would be nice if every supervisor and every employee, for instance, was willing to respect all the others on the job. That situation, of course, is not the case, and never will be. So what do we do?

We respect our co-workers whether we are respected or not. We "do unto them as we would have them do unto us," as the saying goes. We want others to respect us, so we respect them. We know it is our responsibility to respect our fellow laborers, so we do. We begin the process of mutual respect among our co-workers by respecting them first, no matter how they treat us. "Our co-workers" includes anyone we come in contact with on a regular basis at work, whether the president of the company, our immediate supervisor or the lowest-paid employee in the organization.

Treat each person with the same respect you want to be accorded.

AFFIRMATION 5: I will do my work wholeheartedly.

The key word here is *wholeheartedly*. Doing our work half-heartedly keeps us from enjoying it as we should. None of us can enjoy fully what we do only halfway. We must plunge into our work, regardless of what it is, with a sincere desire to enjoy it and a determination to do the very best job we can. That kind of total commitment produces wholehearted work.

Work as if the Lord was your boss. Work as if He was watching over your shoulder every minute of the day. Work to please Him, not other people. Work to please yourself, also, because you know that pleasing yourself will please the Lord.

If you are not working to win the favor of your earthly boss, you will not be disappointed if he fails to compliment you on your work. If you are not working to impress other people, you will not become discouraged if others are not impressed with your work. If you are working wholeheartedly, with a sincere desire to please the Lord, and Him alone, He will always be pleased with you, compliment you, and be impressed with you. You will never be disappointed or discouraged by Him.

The added bonus to this attitude is that others are more likely to notice your work and be impressed with it if you are not working to please them. Try it. It works.

AFFIRMATION 6: I will treat others on the job fairly.

If you are in a position to determine wages and hours for other people, be fair to them. You say that you respect your employees? Then show them respect by providing them fair wages, reasonable hours, and good working conditions. Whatever your position, do everything in your power, appealing to those in authority over you when necessary, to provide fair treatment to those who work under you. Words of respect go unnoticed unless they are backed by tangible proofs.

If you are in the position of an employee, your words of respect must be backed by a fair day's work for a fair day's pay. That basic work ethic is important to the maintenance of good relationships on the job. Thus, it is important to your enjoyment of your work.

Fair treatment works both ways. You expect your employer to give you good pay and reasonable hours. In return, you should expect to give him a full day's work, doing the best job you can. It's a matter of respect. It's also a matter of Christian responsibility.

What if your employer doesn't provide you with what you consider to be fair pay, hours or working conditions? What then? I suggest that you still respect him and still give a full day's work on the job. Who knows? Maybe it will make a difference at the next salary review or wage settlement. Even if it doesn't, you will have done your part in this matter of fair treatment for everyone.

Conclusion

Here then are the six affirmations which you can make that will help you learn to enjoy your work:

I CAN ENJOY MY WORK.

I WILL BE AT PEACE WITHIN MYSELF AT WORK.

I WILL LIVE EACH DAY TO THE FULLEST.

I WILL RESPECT MY CO-WORKERS.

I WILL DO MY WORK WHOLEHEARTEDLY.

I WILL TREAT OTHERS ON THE JOB FAIRLY.

Learn these affirmations. Believe that they are (or can be) true and can match your experience. Realize and accept that these things are your responsibility, first and last. Then say the affirmations repeatedly, day after day, over and over again. Retrain your mind. Begin thinking positively and in accordance with what God desires for you. Then live up to these affirmations daily. Put them into practice. Follow through on them for the rest of your life.

You can *enjoy* your work!

7

Conquer Your Loneliness

Most of us know that famous line from the poet, John Donne: "No man is an island, entire of itself; every man is part of the main." A similar thought is this one from Daniel Webster: "Man is a special being, and if left to himself, in an isolated condition, would be one of the weakest creatures; but associated with his kind, he works wonders."[1] Both of these quotes express the concern of this chapter.

We were not created to live alone. We were meant to enjoy human companionship. We need other people. Marriage is a normal, healthy part of life for most people. Besides marriage – or in addition to marriage – we need other human relationships within our family, among our friends, in the church, on the job. We need the human touch.

When God created Adam, according to the Genesis story, all of creation was not enough to satisfy him. The pleasures he derived from nature, and from the animals whom he had named, were not sufficient. He needed more. Something was missing. "It is not good for man to live alone," God said. And so He created the woman, a human companion for the man. Adam had God for a companion; but even that relationship was not enough. He needed the touch of another human being – someone like

---

[1] From Instant Quotation Dictionary, p. 176.

himself with whom he could share his life, someone to be a part of him. Only with this human companion was Adam's loneliness removed.

A feeling of isolation – loneliness – is one problem which we all face. Perhaps it is more apparent in our generation than in the past. We have so much that should relieve isolation. We have instant communication. We can see and talk with people, almost instantaneously, virtually anywhere in the world. No one is too far away to keep in touch with. Our mobility, especially in America, allows us to cross the country in a few hours to be with those we care about.

In our modern society we have huge cities, and growing populations in small cities. People jostle each other on the sidewalks, barely maneuver themselves through large crowds in shopping malls, impatiently work their way through traffic jams – all the time feeling isolated and alone. Even when we are alone in our homes and apartments, we have people coming into our living room through television, radio and videotapes. We can watch and hear – and almost smell and feel – so many people there with us. But it's not the same. There's no human touch, no warmth, no compassion.

Loneliness affects people in all circumstances of life. People who live alone, whether young or old, widowed, divorced or never married, often feel isolated. But those who are married and share the same table and bed every day can also be lonely. People in large families, both parents and children, often experience isolation even with six other people in the same house with them every day.

If God created us for human companionship, then He did not intend for us to be lonely. So what can we do about it? How do we conquer our loneliness and our feelings of isolation? Can we, in fact, conquer them? Can we ever come to a place in our lives where we are never lonely? Probably not. No one ever fully conquers loneliness. But it can be controlled. We can learn to cope with it, to live mentally healthy and productive lives, even with recurring bouts of loneliness. I believe we can work toward controlling loneliness so that it will never again control us.

What does loneliness have to do with leadership? Being a leader requires that we involve ourselves with other people. It demands that we maintain good human relationships, that we learn to live in positive, self-esteem building ways with our various human companions. Leaders refuse to isolate themselves or to live for long in an isolated existence. They refuse to be cut off from other people. They choose to live with others, in varied relationships, and to involve themselves in other people's lives in constructive, helpful ways. The rest of this chapter will offer some suggestions for overcoming loneliness and establishing and maintaining vital human relationships.

* * * * * * * *

The first three steps toward conquering our loneliness will lay the foundation for the rest of what we do. These first steps deal with our attitude, our motives, our goals in life. They have to do with faith and obedience, the cornerstones of the Christian life.

Realize That You Can't Live Alone

Don't cut yourself off from other people. This statement may seem obvious. If you don't want to be alone, why would you cut yourself off from others? Yet that is exactly what we tend to do. When we are feeling blue and lonely, maybe a little depressed, our tendency is to get off by ourselves and stay there, isolated from other people.

"I don't feel like talking to anyone right now," we say. "I just want to be left alone."

But what we say we want is really just the opposite of what we really need – to talk to someone, to spend some time with another caring, understanding human being.

"My wife and I aren't getting along too well these days."

One reason may be that each of you has cut off the other. There is no attempt to carry on conversation, no willingness to talk through what is happening in your lives right now, no desire for the warmth and compassion of the natural human relationship. No wonder you're lonely.

"My friend Sue and I haven't talked with each other for a month now except to say hello and goodbye. I wonder what's wrong."

Maybe the two of you just need to take time for each other. Make the effort to be with your friend for a while. Take time out of a hectic schedule to restore a healthy friendship. And, in the process, learn to control your loneliness.

Realize that you can't live alone. Don't even try. Don't cut yourself off from the people who can be your companions, those who are, in fact, your partners in marriage, friendship and business. Reach out to them. They need you as much as you need them.

Believe That, Whatever Your Circumstances, You Can Conquer Your Loneliness

This step takes us back to the purpose of our creation. We were created by God for human companionship. We cannot live without it. We need it; and God intends for us to have it. He has provided many possibilities for building solid, healthy relationships with other people. Look for them. Be aware of the people who could be your companions.

Maybe you are widowed after a long and happy marriage. You have no desire to remarry. Fine. There are other possibilities for human companionship. Maybe you are young and single and not ready for marriage; again, there are many possibilities for human companionship that will be fulfilling apart from the sexual involvement (and lifetime commitment) of marriage. Maybe you are married but need other companions outside of the home. Look for the possibilities which God has prepared for you.

Whatever your circumstances – whether you are young or old, married or single, an urban or rural resident, believe that you can control, and even conquer, your loneliness. Coming to that belief is the second step of preparation.

Stay Tuned to the Best Source of Both Divine and Human Companionship: the Church

The New Testament is clear on this point. In the creation, God gave us marriage and the family for companionship. According to the Old Testament, these two institutions were expanded to include various social relationships, particularly that of belonging to a certain people. And from the New Testament, we learn that God – through the new creation that is ours in Christ – has given us a new source for human companionship. It does not replace the others; rather, it encompasses and transcends all others. The Church takes into its reach people of every nation, race, culture and time. It draws into itself the marriage and family relationships, the various social and cultural relationships, and transforms them into something even better.

In the Church, we find people who can provide the human companionship that we need to conquer our loneliness. We also find the divine relationship that will transform and renew every human relationship and enable us to live through all circumstances without being utterly alone. We do not need to ever suffer the devastation of being forgotten, forsaken, abandoned or neglected; for God is always with us through Jesus Christ. That Presence is confirmed and strengthened by the presence of other human beings who have been touched and transformed in the same way.

The Church is the best source of companionship, both human and divine. Don't cut yourself off from it. Stay tuned to that source.

* * * * * * * *

If we will lay the foundation of these first steps, we can go on, in at least six more ways, to learn to control, even to conquer, our loneliness. This list is not exhaustive. I am sure there are other things we can do. But the following are six practical steps, building upon the proper attitude and motive, that will enable us to conquer our loneliness.

Open Up All the Lines of Communication

Isolation comes from being cut off from others. Loneliness is often a result of such isolation. So one remedy is to open up the lines of communication.

If I lived in the mountains miles from anyone else, and the telephone lines were down, I would do everything I could to repair them and restore communication with the outside world. It is the same with our relationships.

We need to talk to people. We also need to listen to what they are saying to us. In fact, if we are to have good communication, we need to listen more than we talk. If we tell others what we are feeling, and then listen to them while they tell us how they feel, if we demonstrate that we are ready to respond to their needs, then the lines of communication are opened. We have taken a giant step toward controlling loneliness.

Be ready to listen and respond to other people. Most of us are always ready to talk about ourselves. Too often we are eager to tell other people all about our problems. Seldom are we as ready to listen to others talk about their needs and concerns. As Christians, we need to learn to respond with whatever help and encouragement is appropriate.

Open up the lines of communication. Don't allow yourself to be cut off from others, especially those who need you most.

Make New Friends

Establish new relationships. Maybe the human companionship you have enjoyed for many years is no longer a possibility for you. Perhaps you're feeling lonely and isolated. You may be a widow or a widower; your spouse is gone, and you must live alone. You may have moved to a new community after many years in one place; your friends and support groups are no longer available to help you. What do you do now?

Perhaps your children have grown up and gone off to college or the military or to start their own families; or maybe you are one of those children yourself and you've moved away to another town or state where you feel very much alone.

In all these circumstances, there is something you can do. Make new friends. Establish new relationships.

You're never too old. You may think you are too far along in life to get married again. Or you may not want to remarry. Those feelings are understandable. You don't have to marry again to build new relationships other than that of husband and wife. You can still get out of the house and be with other people. You can go out and find other lonely widows or widowers with whom you can build good, solid friendships which may last for many years.

You're never alone in your need for human companionship. There are always others around you of your own age who also need someone to talk to, someone to spend time with, perhaps even someone to hold. Look around. Find someone else with similar interests, someone who would like to establish a new relationship.

There are a number of unique ways to go about building new friendships that could bring more excitement or interest to your life. Can't travel? Why not locate a pen pal in another country with whom you can begin to build a friendship? The mission organization of your church, or any of the numerous groups that work to help people overseas, can put you in touch with a foreign pen pal.

There are also foster parent programs in which you can "adopt" (through a small monthly contribution) a child in another part of the world. Why not correspond regularly with that child?

Another idea is to find a local phone partner with whom you share a common interest. Maybe you can't get out much because of poor health, and being housebound is contributing to your loneliness. There are others in your community in the same situation. They are probably looking for companionship just as you are. Find out, through a church or local community group, who else needs that human touch. Call one of those lonely people; strike up a new friendship; become phone partners.

Another suggestion is to write to people who need a word of encouragement. Some people are lonely because they feel they are not important. Why not lift their spirits, and your own, by building their sense of self-esteem?

Make yourself important. Take the time to become something of an expert (or perhaps you already are) on some issue and then write to the person who is responsible for dealing with that issue.

Here is one other idea (and there are many more): *go places you've never gone before*. If you do have a little money and reasonably good health, get out and go someplace you have always wanted to visit. Take a tour; go with a group; strike out with a friend. Get out where people are. Make new friends while you're there. Enjoy life. Be alive. Don't be alone.

Be the Kind of Person You Would Want to Be With

We all want to be with people who are more interested in us than they are in themselves. You've been with people who are absolute bores because all they talk about is their own problems and ailments. Don't ever be that kind of person. No one will want to be with you, either. If you're lonely, be sure to be the kind of person you want to be with.

Sometimes, we create our own isolation by alienating others from us by the way we treat them. Listen to what you say to others; watch how you treat them; examine your relationships to make certain that you are not unconsciously contributing to your own loneliness.

Be Committed to Other People

Refuse to allow anything to break off your relationships, if it is in your power to do so. Sometimes, the other person in a relationship will stubbornly insist on terminating it. Nothing you can say or do will change the situation. In that case, you just have to learn to live with your new circumstances.

But many times, something can be done. Usually, when a relationship is broken, it is because both persons contributed to the breakdown. There must be a long-term commitment (in marriage, a lifetime commitment) to maintaining that relationship, no matter what happens. If the commitment is there for both persons, and if the lines of communication are kept open, most of the time the relationship can be maintained and even strengthened.

This commitment must be one of love. And love is action; it is what we do. We must be committed to being patient and kind, gentle, forgiving, trusting, supportive, honest and everything else that has to do with love. With that kind of commitment, the relationship can usually be saved and loneliness avoided.

When You're Feeling Down and Out, Get Up and Out!

When you're feeling blue, the worst thing you can do is to stay in by yourself. Yet that is exactly what we all tend to do. "I'm just not feeling good today," we tell ourselves. "I don't want to talk to anyone; I'll just stay in." Then we wonder why we're lonely.

When you're feeling that way, and you find yourself saying these things to yourself, that's the time you need to get out with other people and do something, almost anything (within limits), to replace isolation with companionship.

Don't wait for someone else to come your way. Don't sit by the phone and hope that someone will call. Pick up the phone and make the call yourself. Write a letter to a long-time acquaintance. Go by a friend's house and see if he or she wants to go out for a while. Go to church and sit by someone you know (or would like to know); then invite that person to go out for coffee after the service. Go downtown to the donut shop. Go to the park and watch the kids at play. *Do something*, anything, to get out with other people.[2]

Commit Yourself to a Cause/Project/Dream/Goal Which Will Demand That You Be with Others

Loneliness can be created by a feeling of insignificance.

"My life doesn't count for anything. If I died today, no one would ever know that I had lived."

If that is the way you feel, do something about it. What are you interested in? What do you care about in this world? What would you like to see changed? Maybe you have always thought, "Someone should do something about that." *You* do it. *You* change it. *You* go out and lead a crusade to improve things.

Make your life count for something. Make others notice you by doing something noticeable, something worthwhile, something that will benefit others. Dream your most fantastic dream, and then take action to make that dream become reality. Set your highest goal, and work to fulfill it. Find a cause or project that others care about, and head up a group that will be committed to carrying it through to completion.

Involve yourself with other people by becoming part of a group that is committed to a worthy cause.

---

[2] Of course, some people cannot get out at all because of a long-term illness or handicap, for instance. Many of them can at least use the phone or write letters. Those who cannot do any of these things especially need the extra attention people in the churches can give through regular ministries.

Within the Church, there are many important causes and projects. Churches need people who will commit themselves to teaching, visiting, helping with the youth, raising money for mission work, and a dozen other things. Find one that fits your abilities and interests and get involved.

Don't be lonely any more because your life is insignificant. Make it worthwhile.

Conclusion

"It is not good for man (or woman) to be alone." So don't be. God never intended for us to live by ourselves. He created us for human companionship and fellowship. It was for this reason that He gave us marriage, the Church, and numerous other human relationships.

If you're feeling isolated and alone, do something about it. Begin by building a good foundational attitude:

Realize that you can't live alone.

Believe that you can control your loneliness.

Stay tuned to the best source of both divine and human companionship: the Church.

Then do some practical things toward controlling, and perhaps even conquering, your loneliness:

Open up all the lines of communication.

Make new friends and establish new relationships.

Be the kind of person you would want to be with.

Be committed to other people.

Get out when you're feeling down.

Commit yourself to a dream, a cause, a project, a

goal: one which will demand that you be with other people.

Control your loneliness. Perhaps, conquer it. Begin today.

8

Live with the Best

In an earlier chapter, I challenged you to match your highest goal in life to your highest potential for living. We were created to be like God; that calling should be your highest goal – to be like Him. Aim for the best in your life. Why settle for less when you were created for the best?

In the last chapter, I talked about how we were created for human companionship. We cannot live without it. But we also cannot live without divine companionship. We were created for that relationship as well. Just as we should choose good human companions – those who will love us and help us to be better human beings – so we should choose the best in divine companionship.

There really is only one choice, of course. God is the only divine companion we can have; and He is also the best companion we can choose, human or divine. God is our best friend, helper, guide and companion. Why not choose to live with Him for the rest of your life?

In the Creation story, God created Adam and Eve to live with Him, to be companions to Him. They walked with God in the garden in the cool of the day, talking with Him, listening to what He had to say. Adam needed human companionship: "It is not good...to be alone." But Adam and Eve were both created for divine fellowship and companionship. They could not live without it.

When our original parents chose to betray God's trust and to eat from the only tree denied to them, their relationship with their Creator was broken, and death was the result. We will talk more about this subject in the next chapter. For now, we are concerned about the broken relationship. Adam and Eve were forced from the garden where they had enjoyed the immediate presence and knowledge of God. They were kept from re-entering by divine beings who guarded the entrance. But God was still around. Adam and Eve still continued to worship Him. Others after them called upon God's help. Yet never again did human beings enjoy the full companionship with God which Adam and Eve had known at the beginning.

The New Creation story – the Gospel of Jesus Christ – tells us how that full fellowship, relationship and companionship have been restored to us. Reconciliation is the biblical word for this restoration. We have been brought back to God through Christ so that we can enjoy Him, love Him, and live with Him forever. But reconciliation cannot be completed for any one of us until we choose to be reconciled, until we turn back and walk with God.

If I extend my hand to you, and you walk away, shunning my offer of friendship and acceptance, reconciliation cannot occur even though I am ready for it. So it is with God. He has extended His hand; take it. Choose to live with Him now and forever.

* * * * * * * *

Here is an important passage for us to consider as we think about companionship with God:

> **...we have an obligation – but it is not to the sinful nature, to live according to it. For if you live according to the sinful nature, you will die; but if by the Spirit you put to death the misdeeds of the**

body, you will live, because those who are led by the Spirit of God are sons of God. For you did not receive a spirit that makes you a slave again to fear, but you received the Spirit of sonship. And by him we cry, "Abba, Father." The Spirit himself testifies with our spirit that we are God's children. Now if we are children, then we are heirs – heirs of God and co-heirs with Christ, if indeed we share in his sufferings in order that we may also share in his glory.

Romans 8:12-17

On the basis of this passage, I would like to say just two things to you. First,

Make Your Choice

Do you want to live or die? It is your choice, your decision. God has the power of life and death; only in the divine presence can we have life. And only when we live within that presence, through faith in Jesus Christ, are we alive. Apart from that presence, we are dead. To choose God as our companion, to decide to live in His presence, is to choose life over death.

Do you want to live in fear or in hope? The life which God gives us is filled with hope, not fear. We have not received a spirit of fear, but a spirit of power and love. The whole world lives in fear; but the one who believes in Christ, the one who lives with God, lives in hope. There is an anticipation of better things to come, an assurance of good things even now, a confidence that helps us rise above the negative forces, above the tragedies and sorrows of this life. That assurance and confidence is hope; that is what having God as our companion can offer.

Do you want to live apart from God, cut off from your rightful family and home? No one does. No one wants to always be separated from his own family and home. Even when the family experience is bad, there is always the hope that it will improve. Those who had an unhappy home life as children still wish it had been better. We want to be a part of our family, to have a place we can call home. There is a family and home that cuts across the boundary between the human and the divine.

When God becomes our companion, He also becomes our Father in a special way. We become children of God. As Christians, we are now a part of a special family. We have a special home promised to us as members of that family. So choose to live with God and enjoy being home, being part of your intended family, enjoying the benefits of being a member of this great household of faith. It's your choice. Membership in the family of God is yours, if you want it.

Live with Your Choice

Once you have made the choice, once you have accepted God's offer of reconciliation, stick with that choice. Live with the decision you have made. Follow through by living the kind of life that was intended for one who is part of that divine family. Those who belong to this family, those who live in this household, are expected to live in certain ways. Acceptance of that divine lifestyle is part of the choice you are making.

This passage in Romans 8 ends with a word about suffering with Christ in order to be glorified with Him. It talks about being led of the Spirit of God, rather than being controlled by our inner desires. We must choose to trade the passions and selfish desires of our existence for the beautiful desires and fulfilling sacrifice of a life lived in companionship with God. We will be led into a new way of thinking, new attitudes, new ways of acting toward others, a new set of responses to the circumstances of life. In the giving up of what we have known before, we receive a better life, one filled with the very things that were lacking before: love, joy, peace, patience, wisdom, gentleness, confidence, self-esteem. Which life do you choose?

Those who live in constant touch – in companionship – with our heavenly Father are expected to love and honor the whole family and to maintain the good name of both the Father and the family. We have inherited the divine name. The world knows us as those who belong to this family. We have a responsibility in life, then, to bring honor to the family name. We are responsible to love all the members of the family as much as we love the Father Who gave us life and brought us into this new relationship. (And a family who loves one another and honors the family name will also love and honor other people who are outside that family.) Choose to live with us, the family of God.

Those who belong to the Father and the family of faith, have an inheritance held in trust which far exceeds all the riches and pleasures of this earth. If you discovered that a rich relative had died and left you ten million dollars, you would do everything necessary – fulfill every requirement of the will – in order to finally receive the full amount of the inheritance. The Bible uses just such language to describe the inheritance God has provided us through the death of His Son, Jesus Christ. That inheritance is held in trust for us. There are conditions set forth in the "last will and testament" (the New Testament) that need to be fulfilled. There is need for patience as we wait for the appointed time of the final distribution of the proceeds of the trust. But we will receive the full inheritance just as it was promised to us.

Three Aspects of Companionship with God

The choice to live with God, to be a companion to Him and to have Him for our companion, must be understood in three aspects:

> We live with the Father as loving children, obedient to His will, willingly honoring His name and the family name, and loving one another.

> We live with the Son as our brother and companion in suffering and glory, joy and sorrow, testing and victory.

> We live with the Spirit as our constant friend and supporter in all that we do, One Who walks alongside us at all times to comfort, strengthen and enable us to continue.

In all these ways, God is our companion through faith in Christ Jesus. Why not live with the best? Why not choose the best companion possible in this world – and the next? Why not choose – and live with your choice? Choose God. Live with the best. Forever.

9

Live Forever

A 1980s film, "Cocoon," was another in a long line of stories based on the human desire to live forever. People in all ages have looked for – or talked about looking for – some formula for eternal youth, some new discovery, some magic potion that would enable them to avoid aging and death. This desire for immortality has been a dream, a hope, of man throughout recorded history.

We human beings dream about immortality because we were created to live forever. Death was never a part of God's original plan for His highest creation, mankind. Instead, it was, according to the Genesis account, a real possibility for Adam and Eve. In the middle of the garden of Eden stood the Tree of Life. The first human couple were not denied access to that tree; they could have eaten of it and lived on indefinitely. That freedom was given to them in the beginning by their Creator. Only after they had betrayed God's trust and had eaten from the one tree denied to them were they denied access to the tree of life. God had warned them that they would die if they ate of the forbidden tree; and they did die – not physically but spiritually. Spiritual death is separation from God. They lost fellowship with God and access to the tree of life. Eternal life was lost to them. It was no longer a reality, not even a possibility.

When we turn to the end of the Bible, to the book of Revelation, we read of another tree of life and a river of life from which we can freely eat and drink, and therefore live forever. What intervened in human history to reopen the way to eternal life? According to the New Testament, when Jesus Christ died and rose again, He made it possible for every person to regain what had been lost to all mankind – the right to live forever.

Jesus Himself promises eternal life to us. In the eleventh chapter of the Gospel of John we read that Jesus had a friend named Lazarus who was sick and on the verge of death. The sisters of Lazarus, Mary and Martha, sent immediately for Jesus, asking Him to come and heal their brother, just as He had healed many others. But Jesus waited. After several days, He arrived at the family home, but seemingly too late; Lazarus had already died. We know from the rest of the story that Jesus had purposely delayed because He wanted to prove His power over death by restoring life to Lazarus' body. But Martha confronted Jesus about His delay:

> "Lord," Martha said to Jesus, "if you had been here, my brother would not have died. But I know that even now God will give you whatever you ask."
>
> Jesus said to her, "Your brother will rise again."
>
> Martha answered, "I know he will rise again in the resurrection at the last day."
>
> Jesus said to her, "I am the resurrection and the life. He who believes in me will live, even though he dies; and whoever lives and believes in me will never die. Do you believe this?"

"Yes, Lord," she told him, "I believe that you are the Christ, the Son of God, who was to come into the world."

John 11:21-27

These are the words of hope: "...**whoever lives and believes in me will never die....**"(v. 26). In both the Creation and the New Creation, God made us to live forever. No wonder we all share the dream.

Hucksters, con men, frauds – all have tried to sell vain and fearful people on all sorts of schemes for lengthening life. Folklore is full of such tales. But one man alone speaks the truth and truly offers us eternal life. And not for a price, but as a free gift. He charges no money, demands no payment, elicits no vain promises. Eternal life is a free gift, offered without price, to those who will accept it through faith in Jesus Christ.

Step by step, human beings can come out of the darkness of doubt and the shadow of death into the light of hope which the promise of eternal life brings to our existence. All over the world right now, in different ways, in many languages, in a variety of circumstances, people are crying out:

I Don't Want to Die!

Who does? No one, who has a healthy attitude toward this existence, wants to die. No one even wants to grow old; but, of course, the only alternative to growing old is to die. So people want to stay young, thinking somehow that they can avoid death.

We live in fear until we come to Christ. We are afraid of growing old; and we are afraid of death. But in

Christ, fear is taken away. In its place, there is hope. We have the confidence, the assurance of our faith in the promise of God, that we will live on forever and never die. We will go through another passage of life, from this body to another state of existence and to the resurrection. But we will never die.

I hear other people in the world, young and old, cry out:

I Want to Live!

There have been movies, novels, stories of every kind about those who utter this cry of desperation: "I want to live; I don't want to die. I'm not ready for my life to end; there's so much more for me to do!" That attitude is healthy and good. We pity those who have given up on life, those who no longer care whether they live or die. Those without hope are the most needy of all people. We can exist without almost anything except our hope.

It is a sign of good mental health to want to go on living. It is not a vain and useless desire. Rather, it is the dream and hope placed within us all at Creation. That hope is made a reality for each of us in the New Creation. Hang onto hope. Never give it up. Never despair. Eternal life is a "sure thing" for those who believe.

The next step out of the darkness into the light is to have the determination evident in these words:

I Will Live Whatever the Cost!

Most people will – and do – give anything to be able to go on living. Our healthcare bill in America has risen to unbelievable amounts because people want to go on living, to hold on to life, no matter what it costs.

The beautiful thing about God's offer of life is that there is no cost. It's free. You may be thinking, "Oh, but it does cost. We can't have eternal life unless we work for it; we must earn it through constant good works and a severe obedience to God's will." But the Gospel (the Good News) states that, even if we want to, we cannot earn eternal life by our own good works. Either we receive it as a gift, or we can't have it. God has provided it; He offers it to us free; our choice is to accept it or reject it.

Why would anyone reject life? Why would anyone choose death? What we want to hear from people all over the world are these words:

I Am Alive!

I am alive and well, healthy and happy, hopeful and excited about the future. I enjoy life – every day of it. I'm looking forward to life going on forever, whatever that will mean to me.

Too many people wish they weren't alive. They insulate themselves from others, hiding behind their walls of busyness, success, poverty, indifference and a dozen other things. Some rebel against life, refusing to accept and enjoy it, making their existence miserable for themselves and everyone else. Some try to end their existence; and too many succeed. Such people have given up hope, and their despair drives them to a tragic end.

Some people simply ignore life. They just exist, day after day, going to work, going home, eating and drinking, having sex, raising families, but doing nothing that really matters to them. They simply don't care. Apathy is a tragic attitude to have toward life. So many human beings, created by God for continuing life, waste what existence they have by creating for themselves the tragedy of dying without hope.

We humans were created to be alive, truly alive, and to go on living forever. In Christ, in the New Creation, this abundant, eternal life is again a possibility – a reality for those who believe. You don't have to die. You can live – forever. You can have abundant and eternal life, at no cost to you. You can be alive, truly alive, for all eternity.

Part IV:
Make It Work!

Therefore, as God's chosen people, holy and dearly loved, clothe yourselves with compassion, kindness, humility, gentleness and patience. Bear with each other and forgive whatever grievances you may have against one another. Forgive as the Lord forgave you. And over all these virtues put on love, which binds them all together in perfect unity.

Let the peace of Christ rule in your hearts, since as members of one body you were called to peace. And be thankful. Let the word of Christ dwell in you richly as you teach and admonish one another with all wisdom, and as you sing psalms, hymns and spiritual songs with gratitude in your hearts to God. And whatever you do, whether in word or deed, do it all in the name of the Lord Jesus, giving thanks to God the Father through him.

Colossians 3:12-17

1

Start with the Right Attitude

Here is where it all "comes together." How do we make all these fine-sounding ideas work in our lives? If we are agreed that we need to build self-esteem in others to prepare them to be leaders in tomorrow's world, how do we go about it? The answer to these questions is what the last section of the book is all about.

Throughout this section, one thing will be apparent. There is an added bonus to everything we do to build self-esteem in others. When we work to build other people's self-esteem, we increase our own. One effort enhances the other. When we work to increase our own self-esteem, we also build it in others. So it works both ways, as you will discover when you begin to put these ideas into practice.

So where do we start? How do we begin to build self-esteem? There are many good "how-to" books available on this subject, and I certainly can't give you an exhaustive list of things to do that will accomplish this objective. But I would like to give you a start, a place to begin.

The Biblical quotation on the previous page suggests *seven principles for self-esteem builders:*

1. Start with the right attitude.

2. Forgive each other.

3. Love one another.

4. Be peaceful with each other.

5. Be thankful for each other.

6. Learn from each other.

7. Worship the Lord together.

Let's look at these principles one at a time and see how they can help us to build self-esteem in ourselves and others in preparation for future leadership.

PRINCIPLE 1: Start with the Right Attitude

> **Therefore, as God's chosen people, holy and dearly loved, clothe yourselves with compassion, kindness, humility, gentleness and patience.**
> **Colossians 3:12**

Here's a five-piece outfit to put on. Dress yourself up, not in a three-piece business suit, but in this new five-piece spiritual ensemble: compassion, kindness, humility, gentleness and patience. These are five pieces that match, that are coordinated and tailored to fit every personality, every human being. We are not overdressed or faddish when we wear this outfit. Instead, we are in style, always dressed and ready to go out among people, any time and any place. You will fit in everywhere and with everyone when you're attired in this spiritual outfit.

I used to play a lot of ping pong. In that game, the key to success is in the wrist. Strong arm muscles and large swings of the arm only cause problems. If you want to win, you must have the right wrist action in order to put a spin on the ball or to catch the opponent off-guard by hitting the ball in the opposite direction from where you are looking. In ping pong, it's all in the wrist.

Well, in this game of self-esteem building, it's all in the attitude. The key to success in this game of life is our attitude toward God, ourselves and others.

How do you feel about other people? How do you treat them? What is your "attitude aptitude" when it comes to the people you are with each day? How do you feel about your wife, your teenage son or daughter, your boss, your neighbor? Name any person you come into contact with every day: how do you feel about that individual?

Take this *Attitude Aptitude Test*. Answer the questions for each person you can think of:

1. Do I greet _____ with a smile and a sincere "how are you"?   Yes   No
    ____ ____

2. Do I care what's happening in his/ her life?
    ____ ____

3. Am I patient and even-tempered with _____?
    ____ ____

4. Do I *want* to hear what he/she has been doing lately?
    ____ ____

5. Do I give _____ the benefit of the doubt when there is a question about his/her behavior or motives?
    ____ ____

6. Do I think _____ is important, that his/her concerns are as important as mine?
    ____ ____

7. Am I considerate of his/her feelings and time?
    ____ ____

8. Do I readily acknowledge both his/her
   problems *and* mine?   ____ ____

9. When is having problems, do I willingly
   take time to sit down and see what I can
   do to help?   ____ ____

10. When _____ does something
    that angers me, do I react with gentleness
    and patience?   ____ ____

    (Score 10 points for each yes answer. A score of 100
    indicates that you have an excellent attitude apti-
    tude for this relationship.)

Starting with the right attitude is essential for anyone who wants to be a self-esteem builder. You can be one.
It takes work, and time, but you can do it. However, you
can't do it by yourself. You need some outside help. We all
do. We need to find the strength and inner power of a new
life before we can begin to live this kind of life on a consistent, daily basis. It doesn't come naturally to anyone. It
goes against the grain of our natural personality to develop this kind of attitude. We need to find a way to give
ourselves a fresh start.

A fresh start is exactly what God offers us in Jesus
Christ. The good news is that through our faith in Christ,
we can start over. We can find that new beginning. Our
attitudes can be transformed. Our lives can be changed.

In Ephesians 4:22-24 we read about a three-step
entrance into what can become a life of self-esteem building:

Step 1. **...put off your old self, which is being
corrupted by its deceitful desires;**

Step 2. ...**be made new in the attitude of your minds;**

Step 3. ...**put on the new self, created to be like God in true righteousness and holiness.**

Step 2 is the critical one for what we are considering: **...be made new in the attitude of your minds....**(v. 23). Put your faith in Christ. Let God give you a fresh start with your attitude. Learn what kind of attitude you need to have; then let God give it to you. Build up your own self-esteem and that of those around you. Put on this five-piece outfit and get ready to go out and meet and help people.

Compassion

The new self, which we are to put on along with this new attitude, is **...created to be like God...**(v. 24). A few verses later on in that same passage (Eph. 5:1), we read these words: **Be imitators of God, therefore, as dearly loved children....** These are strange and new thoughts to a lot of people, perhaps even to you. How can we be like God? How can we be imitators of God?[1]

One way we can become like God is to become like Christ. Find out what Jesus Christ was like, how He lived, what He taught, how He treated other people. Then follow His example. When we read about Jesus in the Gospels, we find these words:

> **Jesus went through all the towns...teaching...preaching...and healing....When he saw the crowds, he had compassion on them, because they were harassed and helpless....**
>
> **Matthew 9:35-38**

---

[1] We talked about this subject in Chapter 2, Part III. Go back and read it again, if it is still unclear to you how this can happen.

Jesus had compassion for the helpless, the weak, the sinful, for those who doubted, and for those who had turned away from God. Jesus lived a life marked by compassion. He is our example.

Compassion is our response to those who are weak and in need. Whatever their needs or their weaknesses, we respond with the attitude: "How can I help you?" There is no arrogance or contempt or pity toward the person in need. We know that we, too, have been in similar situations ourselves. We, too, have been weak and in need of someone to help us.

We don't look down on people because of their weakness. We treat them with respect and dignity, as if they are deserving of the highest honor, because, in fact, they are. They are all the special products of God's creative power and love. They are human beings, created in the image and likeness of God, created with the potential to be like their heavenly Father through faith in Jesus Christ. They are important, each and every one of them.

Compassion is taking the attitude that every person is important. It is adopting the position of someone who is there simply to help others in their times of need and weakness.

Kindness

Jesus is our example, too, when we consider this attitude. He is the supreme proof of God's goodness, graciousness and kindness to us. In our weakness, our unbelief, our desperate need, God loved us and reached out to us in kindness. He reached out to us when we had slipped off into the darkness, even when we had stepped off intentionally to get away from the light of His love. He reached out to us to give us the best gift anyone could give. He gave us His Son so we could come back to Him and fellowship with Him forever.

In many little ways, God has shown kindness to us. He has given us sun and rain, summer and winter, day and night – all that is needed for our continuing life on this planet. He has given us health in lieu of sickness, wisdom in place of confusion, faith instead of doubt. He has given us family and friends and many who have helped us without our even knowing it. He has been kind in so many ways.

God is our example when it comes to the attitude of kindness. In Jesus Christ, we see it most clearly: when He stopped everything to talk to the children instead of sending them away because He was busy; when He talked to the Samaritan woman at the well – a woman with a bad reputation and what most people considered a worthless life; when He talked to the man whose daughter was at the point of death; and when He talked to Martha after her brother had died. Jesus was kind to people in their times of crisis. When people were hurting, doubting, confused, even when they were insulting to Him, He was kind to them.

A generous spirit and a gracious manner – these are the hallmarks of kindness. Kindness also includes giving others the benefit of the doubt. Take time out of a busy day to notice (and let it be known that you notice) someone else. Have the attitude that what the other person is saying or feeling is important – and show that you think it is. Demonstrate an attitude of kindness.

Humility

We are talking about how to "be made new in the attitude of our minds." Our attitude toward others, we have discovered, should be patterned after God's attitude toward us. And God's attitude toward us is shown most clearly in the life and attitude of Jesus Christ. In Philippians 2:2-5, the Apostle Paul expresses the desire of God for all of His children:

> ...make my joy complete by being like-minded, having the same love, being one in spirit and purpose. Do nothing out of selfish ambition or vain conceit, but in humility consider others better than yourselves. Each of you should look not only to your own interests, but also to the interests of others.
>
> Your attitude should be the same as that of Christ Jesus.

Then the passage goes on to tell how Christ was equal with God, but gave up His right to power and glory in order to become a man. As a man, He gave up His life as a sacrifice for us. His example of total humility is our pattern and role model for forming a new attitude.

Humility is often misunderstood. Christ could give up everything – in total humility – only because He knew Who He was. While He was on earth, He said of Himself: "I AM; I am one with the Father; I am the light of the world; I am the resurrection and the life; I am the way, the truth, and the life." Jesus Christ knew that He was important. He knew Who He was and why He was here and where He was going. He had perfect self-esteem. And His self-esteem allowed Him to feel that others were important, too. In fact, He adopted the attitude that the desperate needs of human beings were more important than His own needs and feelings. So He sacrificed everything for the sake of others.

That spirit of self-sacrifice is true self-esteem and true humility.

Christ is our example. Like Him, we can be humble and still be filled with positive self-esteem. We can sacrifice our lives for others, knowing that we are important, and that they are important, too. We can have the assurance of who we are and where we are going; and we can have the compassion and kindness, augmented by humility, that motivates us to surrender everything to the goal of helping others. Humility is not looking down on ourselves as inferiors, nor looking up to others as though they are better than we; rather, true humility is holding others up in their time of need, even if it means losing ourselves and our position of strength in the process.

Holding others up, even at our own expense – that attitude is true humility.

Gentleness

Every one of these attributes builds on those that come before it. If we have compassion, kindness and humility, then we will be gentle toward others. Gentleness is the natural extension of these other virtues.

Anyone who is even a little familiar with the story of Jesus of Nazareth knows that He was a gentle man. There were times when He chose to publicly demonstrate the anger of God toward self-righteous, hypocritical religious leaders. But toward people who acknowledged their weakness and need, He was always gentle.

Gentleness is consideration. We need to be considerate of other people's feelings. We must be considerate of their circumstances, knowing that because of their human weaknesses most people are drawn, almost against their will, into difficult situations. We must be considerate of their weakness, because we know that we also are weak in other ways.

Consideration is the opposite of arrogance, contempt or pity. It is a gentle spirit toward others who are not always gentle toward us, toward others, or even toward themselves.

Hard times make some people hard. Violent, angry people are the products of a violent, angry world. Tragedy and sorrow and grief have made many people defensive and hurtful. But all these people are hurting. They are weak. They are in need. One of their greatest needs is for others to respond to them in gentleness.

Be considerate. Be gentle. Build up the self-esteem of hurting people.

Patience

As with the other four attitudes we have examined, patience is best learned by considering how patient God has been with us. Like little children, or perhaps more like rebellious teenagers, we have so often tried God's patience. We have been selfish and self-centered. We have doubted God and betrayed His trust in us. By our refusal to let Him have control of our lives and problems, we have demonstrated our lack of faith in God's trustworthiness. We have refused to listen to what He wants us to know, and we have been determined to live our own lives our own way, in spite of what we know God wants us to do.

We have tried God's patience to the breaking point; yet God has always remained patient and loving and caring toward us. He bears with us in our weakness and even in our selfishness. He cares about us, despite our unbelief and even our rebellion. God loves us. He knows our weakness and our sin. Still, He loves us; and He continues to remain patient with us.

God is our example of perfect patience. We should bear with others in their weakness, as He has done with us in ours. We should consider their failures, their lack of strength and their stubbornness in light of our own. Has anyone done any more to try our patience than what we have done to try the patience of God? Has anyone hurt us – by refusing to listen to us – any more than we have hurt God by our steadfast refusal to listen to His Word? What have others done to us that we have not done to God? Consider our own selfishness, lack of trust, jealousy, pride and stubbornness. If God has forgiven it all, if He has been patient with us through it all, what have others done to us that disqualifies them from our patience and forgiveness?

Conclusion

Build up self-esteem in others by starting with the right attitude. Put on this five-piece outfit and be ready to go out to meet and help other people. Develop these attitudes: compassion, kindness, humility, gentleness and patience. Let all your words and thoughts and actions toward others be motivated by these positive attitudes.

And remember the added bonus: when we work at building self-esteem in others, we increase our own. When we adopt these attitudes in our relationships with other people, we grow in our self-esteem as we become *self-esteem builders.*

Exercises for the Self-Esteem Builder

1. Choose one person in whom you want to build up self-esteem. It may be a child, a spouse, a friend or a co-worker.

   List everything good you can think of in that person's life – every strong point, strength of character, talent and good deed he or she has ever performed.

   a. Thank God for each item on the list – and for the person who has those good points.

   b. Tell the other person what you have done; congratulate and encourage him or her to continue being the kind of person you have described.

   c. (Now choose someone else and repeat this process.)

2. Choose one person toward whom you have felt contempt or pity (or perhaps a person who represents those toward whom you have held such feelings).

   Find three ways to show compassion toward that person.

3. For one week, keep a pocket journal in which you jot down every one of your remarks or actions that could be described as unkind, angry, impatient, abusive or violent.

   At the end of the week, write next to each entry at least one way you could or should have reacted differently.

4. Compare yourself, in writing, to another person with whom you have a close relationship (child, spouse, co-worker, etc.). In two columns complete these sentences in as many ways as possible:

I am...   He/she is...

I am good at...   He/she is good at...

I am not so good at...   He/she is not so good at...

I wish he/she would...   He/she wishes I would...

Share these comparisons with the other person and discuss your feelings about what you have written. Ask the other person to do the same.

5. Choose *just one* person whose self-esteem you will work consistently to build up during the next six months. Write down 10 ways you plan to accomplish this goal. Then begin.

2

Forgive Each Other

I am convinced that the greatest threat to our emotional and spiritual health is bitterness and the accompanying feelings of guilt and shame. The combined power of these negative forces threatens our health and even our life. The combination of bitterness/resentment toward others and guilt/shame toward ourselves is the single most potent factor keeping us from a healthy self-esteem. There is only one cure for the cancer which eats away at the tissue of our emotional and spiritual lives. That cure is forgiveness.

PRINCIPLE 2: Forgive Each Other

In regard to this principle, the key quotation is Colossians 3:13:

> **Bear with each other and forgive whatever grievances you may have against one another. Forgive as the Lord forgave you.**

Another relevant Biblical quotation is this one from the book of Ephesians:

> **"In your anger do not sin": Do not let the sun go down while you are still angry, and do not give the devil a foothold....**
>
> **...do not grieve the Holy Spirit of God, with whom you were sealed for the day of redemption. Get rid of all bitterness, rage and anger, brawling and slander, along with every form of malice. Be**

> **kind and compassionate to one another, forgiving
> each other, just as in Christ God forgave you.**
> **Ephesians 4:26,27,30-32**

From these two passages, we find that there are two sides to forgiveness: God has forgiven us, and we are to forgive others. These two aspects of forgiveness come together in this way: we can forgive others just as God, in Christ, has *already* forgiven us. When we discover this two-sided truth of forgiveness, and begin to experience both sides of it, we will be able to enjoy healthy self-esteem. Emotionally and psychologically, we will be healthier. We will begin to escape the negative force of bitterness and resentment toward others. And we will escape the bondage of our own guilt and shame. What a fantastic potential for new life!

It was this realization that led to the reformation of the Church in the 16th century. Martin Luther, especially, had struggled for years with his own guilt. Despite the fact that he was a believer, even a priest, he could not shake off the feeling that God had not yet fully accepted him. He wanted, more than anything else, to find peace with God and to know that he was acceptable in God's sight. No rigorous devotion, no rigid adherence to religious duty, no amount of prayer or confession or penance was able to provide him this assurance of forgiveness and acceptance.

Finally, Luther rediscovered the New Testament truth that God has *already* forgiven us through Jesus Christ, simply through divine grace. As Luther read the books of Romans and Galatians, he began to realize the simple promise of God: if we believe in Jesus Christ as the One Who died for our sins and as the One Who has provided everything necessary for our forgiveness and salvation, then – by the grace of God – we are forgiven of all our sin and accepted by God. For the first time Luther saw that we are saved by the grace of God through faith in His Son Jesus. That rediscovery of the Gospel, of the simple truths of salvation, led Luther and many others into what is now called the Reformation. That discovery – that simple truth – is the core of our heritage in the Protestant Evangelical churches today.

The tragedy is that, while preaching it from our pulpits Sunday after Sunday, we have neglected it in our everyday living. We have bound up our people in rules and regulations, traditions and customs, rigid doctrines and unbending beliefs. We have preached more about the power of sin than the power of grace. We have taught people to condemn themselves because of what they have done and to continually struggle to overcome their sinfulness by righteous behavior. Clean living and belief in the "right" doctrines have become the hallmarks of the American Protestant traditions.[1]

We need a new reformation. We need to change the way we preach, even the way we think. We need to rediscover – again – the simple truth of the Gospel, that we have *already* been forgiven in Christ and need only to accept our forgiveness and live in freedom and joy.

That life of simplicity, freedom and joy is the life we have been called to in Christ. But it is not the life which many Christians are living or many preachers are proclaiming.

---

[1] And through the missionary movement of the American Protestant churches, especially, we have spread this cultural religion around the world.

In the New Testament, we are nowhere commanded to ask for the forgiveness of our sins. Only in what we call the Lord's Prayer (Matt. 6:9-13) are we even taught to ask for forgiveness. And there our forgiveness is linked to the phrase, "as we forgive." The statement, "Forgive us, Lord, in the same way we forgive others," is, in fact, more of a commitment of ourselves to forgive others than a request for God's forgiveness of us.

What the New Testament does teach us is to believe in Christ, confess our sins, and receive or accept the forgiveness that is offered to us in Him. It is not so much a matter of *asking for* forgiveness as it is of *receiving* forgiveness. The message is: "Believe in Jesus Christ as your Savior, confess your sins openly to Him, and accept the forgiveness which God offers you."

You are forgiven.

There is tremendous power in these words. There is power to free us from our guilt and shame. There is power to free us from self-condemnation and self-pity. There is power to free our minds from the bondage caused by our fear of being condemned for what we have done or failed to do. In these simple words – *you are forgiven* – there is power to make us free and to fill us with joy.

When we are set free from the fear of God's condemnation, we can be free from our self-condemnation. Many people are mentally and emotionally ill because they cannot forgive themselves. Some people have, in fact, committed some terrible sin for which they bear enormous guilt. Some others only imagine that they have sinned. But the effect is the same: they continue to condemn themselves. Often, people live in guilt or shame because of what they perceive to be their failure as parents. Whatever the sin – real or imagined – they suffer for years under a terrible load of guilt and shame. All because they cannot forgive themselves.

The acceptance of God's forgiveness – His free and unconditional forgiveness for *everything* we have done – frees us from this burden of self-condemnation, guilt and perpetual shame. We are free! We are forgiven.

The Other Side of Forgiveness

The second side of this matter of forgiveness depends on the first. That is, our ability to forgive others depends on our having received the free gift of God's forgiveness for ourselves. But once we have accepted that forgiveness, we are under orders to forgive others in the same way.

If there is any command concerning forgiveness in the New Testament, it is that we forgive others as we have been forgiven. The Lord's Prayer request ("Forgive us our debts, as we forgive our debtors") suggests as much. Other teachings of Jesus in the Gospels make it abundantly clear. (See Matt. 18:15-35; Mark 11:22-25.) And other New Testament passages, such as the ones at the beginning of this chapter, clarify it further: *we are to forgive others as God has forgiven us.*

Think about it. What has God forgiven in your life? Just for your own use, make a list of 25 things for which God has forgiven you. Now think of any one person whom you find it hard to forgive. List everything that person has done to you. Compare the two lists and then answer this question: what has that person done to you to keep you from forgiving him or her, compared to what you have done to God for which He has already forgiven you? If God can forgive all our sins against Him, why can't we forgive the offenses of other people against us?

What does forgiveness have to do with self-esteem? How does all of this discussion about the Gospel, grace, and divine forgiveness relate to our subject of building up self-esteem in other people?

Self-esteem is the belief that we are important; as such, it makes us feel good about ourselves. But guilt and shame over past sin or failure keeps us from feeling good about ourselves (or anyone else). It keeps us bound up as prisoners of our memories. We keep going over in our minds what we did wrong, how terrible we are, how there is nothing we can ever do to make up for our mistake or failure.

That last statement is true. There is nothing we can ever do to "make up" for our past sins. But the good news is that we don't have to. We don't have to do some kind of penance or good work to try to atone for our sins. Jesus Christ has already done everything for us. God offers us – with no strings attached – the gift of forgiveness, inner joy, peace and freedom from guilt for the rest of our lives.

The assurance of our forgiveness frees us from the bondage of shame and guilt so we can begin to live with a positive self-esteem which is rooted in who we are in Christ.

What does forgiveness have to do with building self-esteem in others? Our lack of forgiveness toward others encourages guilt or shame in them. When we refuse to forgive others, we encourage them to condemn themselves for who they are or for what they have done. If we don't forgive them, they are continually reminded of the past and forced to live under its condemnation. So our lack of forgiveness of other people destroys any self-esteem they may have or hope to build.

But the opposite is also true. If we forgive others, we encourage them to forgive themselves. When we forgive other people for what they have done to us, we help them leave the past behind and live in a joy-filled present with hope for the future. Our forgiveness assures them of God's forgiveness, which sets them free from their memories and the bondage of past sins. They begin to realize that they are important. They believe that they are worth something after all. They know that what they did is over and done with. They are ready to go on living in this new life which is ours in Christ. They begin to feel good about themselves. Their self-esteem is strengthened.

Conclusion

Remember: inner freedom comes when we have the assurance that we are forgiven in Christ, and when we have forgiven others as God forgave us.

You are forgiven.

You are free.

Go in peace.

Exercises for the Self-Esteem Builder

1. For your eyes only, make a list of everything you have ever done for which God needs to forgive you (limit 25). Now thank God that He has *already* forgiven each and every one of those sins through Christ.

2. List five persons who have hurt you or offended you in some way. Write down how it happened. What did that person do?

   a. Thank God that He has forgiven each of these persons.

   b Tell God that you forgive each one of them.

   c. Go to each person and say, "I forgive you." (*Caution:* If the other person is not aware that he or she has offended or hurt you, be careful about this step. You don't want to create problems where there are none.)

   d. The next time you experience feelings of anger or resentment toward any of these persons because of something which you have already forgiven, say to yourself:

      "I have already forgiven that offense. I will continue to forgive _____ if anything else happens. I will not be controlled by these feelings of anger/resentment. I am free because I am forgiven, and I have forgiven _____."

3. Practice these (or similar) phrases that will help you voice your willingness to forgive another person:

"I forgive you."

"That's all right. Forget it."

"There's nothing to apologize for. Really. You didn't do anything wrong."

"I love you. I'm not hurt or angry; I just didn't understand, that's all."

4. For one week, keep a pocket journal in which you record each time you are hurt or offended by what someone else says or does. At the end of the week, write next to each item at least one other way you could have understood or reacted to the situation that would have kept you from becoming resentful, angry or hurt. Decide to begin reacting in these ways from now on.

3

Love One Another

The process of building self-esteem in others is complex. It cannot be achieved by following a step-by-step procedure. Instead, everything must be done at once. Each of these seven principles is intricately related to the others. This third principle, especially, includes all the other six.

PRINCIPLE 3: Love One Another

**And over all these virtues put on love, which
binds them all together in perfect unity.**
Colossians 3:14

Love is inclusive. To show love, we must begin with the right attitude. We need to have the combined attitudes of compassion, kindness, humility, gentleness and patience. When we do, we are well on our way to living in love toward others, and on our way to becoming self-esteem builders. Forgiveness, of course, is an essential part of love. We forgive those we love; and we love those we forgive. One is incomplete without the other.

But what is love?

* How can we understand what love is?

* How can we know what it is like?

In this chapter, we will answer these two questions in part. Whole books have been devoted to these questions, and we certainly will not be able to provide any exhaustive explanation of love. But we can come up with some practical insights into how to love others, and thus become better self-esteem builders.

PART A: How Can We Understand What Love Is?

In the New Testament, the first letter of John (1 John) *is* the book of love, making it clear to us that we must love others if we are to claim the name of Christ and call ourselves Christians. As we consider this book, we can come up with six affirmations that will guide us and strengthen us in our search for love.

AFFIRMATION 1: I will love because I am loved.

Everyone knows the Golden Rule: treat others as you want them to treat you. But the other side of that statement is also true: we treat others as we are treated. We react toward others as they act toward us. If we are yelled at, we yell back. If we are hit, we hit back. If we are cheated, we cheat others. At least, that rule seems to describe the natural way of life for most human beings, the way we most often act and react.

The positive side of this rule is that if we are treated with love, we will usually return love. If we are forgiven, it is easier for us to forgive. If others treat us gently, we are more likely to be gentle ourselves. So when we are loved by someone else, when we experience true love, it becomes possible for us to love others. In support of this truth, consider these scriptures:

> **How great is the love the Father has lavished on us, that we should be called children of God!...**
>
> **1 John 3:1**

> **This is how we know what love is: Jesus Christ laid down his life for us....**
>
> **1 John 3:16**

> This is how God showed his love among us:
> He sent his one and only Son into the world that we
> might live through him. This is love: not that we
> loved God, but that he loved us and sent his Son as
> an atoning sacrifice for our sins.
>
> 1 John 4:9,10

> We love because he first loved us.
>
> 1 John 4:19

God loves us and has proved His love for us by the death of His Son, Jesus Christ. This truth is at the core of the Gospel. It is at the heart of any theology that seeks to give us a foundation for building self-esteem. God loves us. What better reason could we have for feeling good about ourselves than the fact that God loves us? What better reason could we find for loving others than our knowledge that God loves us – and them?

When we have believed in God, accepted His love and experienced the daily pleasures of that love, we are able to love others freely. *God's love frees us to love others.* We are no longer bound up in our fear of being unloved because we know that we are loved. We are no longer moved to anger, hatred or resentment because of how others have treated us; rather, we are moved to love others because we have been loved ourselves: **We love because he first loved us** (1 John 4:19).

AFFIRMATION 2: I will love because I am God's child.

My generation seems to be locked into a perpetual quest for our identity. "Who am I?" is the question that continues to be explored (but never answered) in so much of our music, literature and poetry. The search for personal identity is a tragic pursuit, though, because that identity has already been revealed to us. It is no secret. We were created to be the children of God. In Christ, we have been offered the new creation which fulfills our intended purpose. In Jesus Christ – through faith in Him – we are now fully the children of God. We know Who our Father is. We know that we belong to a certain family – the family of God. We know where our home is and what our inheritance will be. All these things have been settled for us. There is no quest, no search for identity; that is not necessary. The answer is already there; it only needs to be accepted.

We can deny our heritage. We can reject our family. We can leave home and never return. We can be stubborn and proud and refuse to ever accept our rightful place in the family. But what a tragic waste of life. What a sad life to lead.

Accept your place in the family as a child of God. Believe these words of scripture:

> **How great is the love the Father has lavished on us, that we should be called children of God!**
>
> **1 John 3:1**

> **...love comes from God. Everyone who loves has been born of God and knows God.**
>
> **1 John 4:7**

> **. . . God is love. Whoever lives in love lives in God, and God in him.**
>
> **1 John 4:16**

Now the relationship between love and being a child of God becomes clear:

I will love others because I am God's child. God is love; I can live in love because I live in God. Love comes from God; I have been born of God and therefore I can love others. Love has become a possibility – even a reality – because I am now God's child.

It works the other way, too:

Because I love others, I know that I am a child of God. Because each day I show my love for others by the way I treat them, I know that I have been born of God and that I live in God. My daily experience of love and my relationship to God are locked together by a bond that cannot be broken. I will love others because I am a child of God.

AFFIRMATION 3: I will love because others are in need.

The question we are answering is: how can we understand what love is? Part of the answer to that question is that we understand by doing. Understanding of anything comes partly by study and partly by experience. We don't learn math without doing exercises, working out the problems according to the principles we have studied. We learn music by studying the principles and then practicing them every day. Almost any subject can be mastered by first studying the principles of it and then practicing them by solving appropriate problems. Love is the same way.

Love can be mastered only by first learning the principles and then by putting them into practice by solving problems at hand. For instance, hear these words:

If anyone has material possessions and sees his brother in need but has no pity on him, how can the love of God be in him? Dear children, let us not love with words or tongue but with actions and in truth.

1 John 3:17,18

Love is understood only when our words of love are combined with our actions of love. We must prove what we say by what we do.

If others are in need, we respond to their needs to the limits of our resources. This response is love in action. The need may be financial: the person may need clothing, food, rent, medicine, lodging, etc. The need may be emotional: the person may need counseling, supportive friends, prayer, a listening ear. The need may be spiritual: the person may need the truth of the Gospel, or a friend to help him believe, or prayer for salvation. Whatever the need, we will respond to it to the limits of our resources because we love. When we do that, we have begun to understand love.

AFFIRMATION 4: I love, so I know that I have eternal life.

We now turn to the outcome of our love in order to understand it better. The source of life – its origin and foundation – is found in God's love, and in being a child of God, responsive to the needs of others. But what is the result of love in our lives?

This affirmation rests on this scripture:

We know that we have passed from death to life, because we love our brothers.

1 John 3:14

The assurance of salvation, as Christians have traditionally called it, rests in part on love. Our love for others – expressed in actions as well as words – produces a confidence in us that we do have eternal life. God's grace, working through our faith, has given us a new life in

Christ. And our love, working in our daily lives, is the proof of this new life. It fosters a new assurance that our regeneration has actually taken place, that it is real.

How could I love others unless I know God? Unless God has changed me, as He promised to do, how could I find it in myself to love others as I do? Unless God's grace, working through my faith, has transformed me into a new person, how could I possibly love other people and respond to their needs in the way I am now doing? So the conclusion is that God has indeed changed me and has given me a new life. I know that I have passed from death to life because I love others.

AFFIRMATION 5: I love, so I have confidence before God.

Because we love others, we have both the assurance of eternal life and the confidence that God does (and will always) accept us. Hear the words of this scripture:

> ...if our hearts do not condemn us, we have confidence before God and receive from him anything we ask, because we obey his commands and do what pleases him. And this is his command: to *believe* in the name of his Son, Jesus Christ, and to *love* one another as he commanded us. (emphasis mine)
>
> **1 John 3:21-23**

The interaction of faith and love is at the heart of the New Testament. There is no true faith without love; and there is no true love without faith. They go together; they are inseparable. One is the test of the other. If we love others, it is the evidence of our faith in God. If we have faith in God, through Jesus Christ, it is the proof of our love. If we believe in God and love Him, we will also love others;

and our love for others is the test of our faith and love for God.

God will accept us now and forever if we believe in Jesus Christ and love one another. These two actions are His command, His will. If we do His will, we will be pleasing to Him, and He will accept us, which is proved by the fact that He hears us and that our hearts do not condemn us. If we are at peace within our hearts, and our prayers are heard, if we have the assurance that God has accepted us, then we can have full confidence and hope both for this life and for the one to come.

AFFIRMATION 6: I love, so I have no fear.

Hope, too, is an outcome of love. Fear is opposed to hope, and hope overcomes fear. Love is the source of such power:

> **There is no fear in love. But perfect love drives out fear, because fear has to do with punishment. The man who fears is not made perfect in love.**
>
> **1 John 4:18**

Love drives out fear. Remember that truth. Believe it. Live by it. Do you want to live each day in hope and positive expectation of the good things which tomorrow will bring? Do you want to escape your fear of what might happen tomorrow, or the day after, or on the final day of judgment? Do you want to live free of fear, to live in hope that God loves you and has accepted you, that He will fulfill all His good promises to you? The key is love.

God's love for us, experienced through faith in Jesus Christ, drives out fear. Our love for God, offered up in faith, drives out fear. Our love for others, which is the natural extension of our love for God, drives out fear. Our love for God, fulfilled in our actions of love toward others, drives out fear.

Love – and be set free of fear.

PART B: How Can We Know What Love Is?

By this question, I mean, "How can we know what we should be like if we really do love other people?" Is there some way to test our actions against the "real thing" to see how we measure up? Whose criteria will we use in determining whether our treatment of others is evidence of authentic love?

The best answer is not the best solution. If God is love, then God's actions toward us are the best test of what love is like. But God's action is a difficult thing to determine. We all have different ideas of just what it is that God does – or whether any particular event was an act of God. Was that occurrence God's doing? Or just our doing? Or someone else's doing? Or did it just "happen"? Again, it is difficult to establish the criteria for judging God's actions.

The New Testament says that Jesus Christ is the complete expression of God's love. If we study His life – how He lived, what He taught, how He treated others – we can begin to perceive the criteria we need to determine how we measure up to the love of God. But, once again, there are various interpretations of the Gospels and differing ideas on the accuracy of what we read in them. Even if we accept every word as true and accurate, the interpretations and applications can differ greatly. So what can we do?

How can we know what true love is like? Isn't there a simpler, more straight-forward way to determine the characteristics and qualities of God-like love? Isn't there some list in the scriptures that sets forth the attributes of love so we can know how we should live, how we should act toward others? As a matter of fact, there is.

One chapter in the New Testament is commonly referred as the "Love Chapter." It is 1 Corinthians 13. In verses 4 through 8 of that chapter, we do find a list of the characteristics of love. It's not an exhaustive list. There is much more that could be added to it, and the rest of the scriptures do add much more to it. But it is a good starting place in our quest to define authentic, God-like love.

If we can understand this description of love, and live up to it, the other lessons of life will be much easier. If we will do the things outlined in this chapter, we will find ourselves loving others whom we thought we could never love. If we will follow through with these actions of love, then those we say we love will discover something in us that they never knew was there.

Love Is Patient and Kind

This is the essence of love. It is the litmus test; dip your love in it and see if it's the "real thing." Every word, every action, every thought can be tested against this two-fold definition. You say that you have love? Then place it on the balance scales and place patience and kindness on the other side. What happens? Love is, first and always, patient and kind.

The next seven tests reveal what love is *not*. These negative attitudes come from a self-centered heart and mind and are opposed to love. These statements indicate the things which should not be in your life.

Love Does Not Envy

It is not jealous. If some other person receives more recognition than you do – or receives the recognition you thought belonged to you – you will not be jealous or envious. Rather, you will sincerely congratulate the other person and go on.

Love Does Not Boast

It is not always telling about the latest accomplishment or trip or imagined success without the slightest concern for what's happening in the lives of others.

Love Is Not Proud

It is never arrogant, vain or conceited. We do need a healthy self-esteem, as we have said throughout this book. But this kind of egotistical, self-centered pride is not healthy. An ego that has grown too large will explode and destroy both that person and those around him or her.

Love Is Not Rude

We have learned too well from a steady diet of television sit-coms (situation comedies). We have become a generation of amateur comedians who think it's funny to "cut people down," to belittle, or to be just plain rude.

Love Is Not Self-Seeking

Love is concerned for God first and others second. In that balanced concern, a healthy self-esteem is generated within ourselves. We do not disregard our own needs;

but we merge our needs with God's will and the needs of others as we live a balanced life of love.

Love Is Not Easily Angered

As *The Living Bible* notes in verse 5a, love is **...not irritable or touchy...** Now, that truth hurts. Who is not at times touchy or irritable? Perhaps this way of saying it is best: Love **...will hardly even notice when others do it wrong** (v. 5b TLB). That attitude will keep us from being resentful and bitter; that attitude is love.

Love Keeps No Record of Wrongs

One follows the other. We will hold no grudges against others if we do not even notice when they do us wrong. But if we do notice, and if we do get angry, we can still decide to forgive and to say, "I will not hold anything against that person."

Here is still another important part of love:

Love Does Not Delight in Evil,
But Rejoices with the Truth

We can never be content if the one we love is doing wrong, or is not right in his or her life. Those two things are not necessarily the same. Many people never really do anything wrong. They don't lie or cheat or murder or steal or commit adultery. But they are not right in their lives either. They don't believe in the Lord. They have never committed their lives to God. They are self-centered, out to get everything they can from life.

Love is *not* blind. Love sees what the other person is doing. Love sees where the other person is in life, spiritually and emotionally. Love cares enough about the other person to try to correct the wrong – through prayer, constant attention to the other's need, gentle persuasion, continual and open communication and, when necessary, firm discipline (especially with children). "Tough-love" is what some are calling it now.

The last four characteristics of love in this passage are summed up in the opening words of verse 8: *love never fails*. Love never gives up; it never quits on anyone. Do you have a difficult child? Do you have a spouse who does not return your love? Do you know someone who won't yield to any of your efforts to show your love and concern? Don't give up; keep on loving and loving and loving – love without end.

Love Always Protects

Traditionally, men have always thought they were supposed to protect women. But it is (and always has been) both men and women who need to protect each other. Such protection is not only physical and financial, it is also emotional and spiritual. All persons are weak in their own individual ways and need some kind of protection provided for them by the ones with whom they share their lives.

Love Always Trusts

Talk to the one you love. Tell him or her your deepest feelings. Trust that person to understand. Trusting is tough; it has never been easy. And it doesn't necessarily get easier with the passing years of marriage, for instance. In fact, it gets harder, sometimes, because of the memories of those occasions when things weren't so good between you and your mate. But love always comes back to the present and dares to trust again.

Love Always Hopes

Always expect the best *in* the other person, and always expect the best *for* the other person. Hope and expectation go together. Hope for the best for others, and do all you can to make the best happen.

Love Always Perseveres

This thought brings us back to the opening phrase: *love never fails.* Keep on keeping on in every circumstance of life. You don't want the other person to give up on you when you are weak or have failed, so don't give up on him or her.

Here, then, is our checklist for testing our actions and attitudes against what love is really like. If your present actions and attitudes don't seem to match up very well, then turn these statements into faith-affirmations.[1]

Here they are again. See how you are doing in your "love life."

_____ *Love Is Patient and Kind*

_____ *Love Does Not Envy*

_____ *Love Does Not Boast*

_____ *Love Is Not Proud*

_____ *Love Is Not Rude*

_____ *Love Is Not Self-Seeking*

---

[1] An affirmation is a statement of truth. As I use the term "faith-affirmation," I am referring to a statement of something that should be true in your life or something that you expect to become true. For example: "I will love others; therefore, I will be patient and kind."

_____ *Love Is Not Easily Angered*

_____ *Love Keeps No Record of Wrongs*

_____ *Love Does Not Delight in Evil,
But Rejoices with the Truth*

_____ *Love Always Protects*

_____ *Love Always Trusts*

_____ *Love Always Hopes*

_____ *Love Always Perseveres*

_____ *Love Never Fails*

No one is perfect. We all have a long way to go in our growth toward becoming self-esteem builders. Remember what I said earlier in the book. There's a double bonus in being a self-esteem builder: in the process of building up self-esteem in others, our own self-esteem is strengthened. That statement is especially true here. In order to build up self-esteem in others, we have to love them. But we can love them when our self-esteem is strong.

So strengthen your self-esteem by exercising your love. Follow through with the exercises at the end of this chapter. Work at them each day for a month. Then test yourself again. I guarantee you will be stronger and more healthy in love and self-esteem.

Exercises for the Self-Esteem Builder

1. In Part A, memorize the verses from 1 John and match them up in your mind with the affirmations.

2. Memorize the affirmations in Part A and repeat them at least 10 times each day for a month. (Apply them to what you are doing throughout the day.)

3. Spend 15 minutes each day for a month reading through the Gospels (Matthew, Mark, Luke and John in the New Testament). Look for, and write down in your own words what you discover about, the ways that Jesus acted in love toward others.

4. For one month, keep a journal in which you write down how you think you are doing in loving others. Each day, select one item from the checklist and test all you do throughout the day against that one criterion. Then at the end of the day, write down your feelings. You can go through the whole list at least twice in a month.

5. Turn each checklist item into a faith-affirmation, especially if you feel weak in that area. For instance, if you tend to be touchy and irritable, say these words throughout the day: "I am not easily angered." Whenever things get tough and you are tempted to react harshly, say these words again as if they were true for you – and you will soon discover that they *are* true for you. Repeat this exercise with each area in which you think you are weak.

4

Be Peaceful with Others

We have no greater need in our lives than that of peace. Even the world recognizes this fact. Peacemaking has become a widely accepted practice in our time. We can see that if civilization as we have known it is to continue, war must become a thing of the past. Even conventional wars have become too destructive, and a nuclear war would destroy us all. Our world could not survive widespread nuclear warfare and still maintain any semblance of our present civilization. So finding ways to establish lasting peace has become a major political pastime among the nations.

The issue of peace, though, extends down through the layers of society to the family and individual levels as well. For the purpose of this book, this personal peace issue is the one we must face. How can we live peacefully with others in marriage, in the family, on the job, among our friends, in the Church or in any other human relationship? How is it possible to live peacefully with other people?

PRINCIPLE 4: Be Peaceful with Others

Let the peace of Christ rule in your hearts, since as members of one body you were called to peace....

Colossians 3:15

This principle is the challenge, the call to action for those who would become self-esteem builders. Let me give you *five principles for peaceful living* which I believe can help us realize this goal.

PRINCIPLE 1: Be at Peace with God

No human relationship is complete in the absence of a good divine-human relationship. We cannot live peacefully with others if we are not at peace with God. Each person must find the inner peace that comes from the divine-human relationship before he or she will be fulfilled in any human relationship.

An old saying urges us to "make peace with God" before our death. The idea is that we will not want to face God at the judgment without first having made our peace with Him here on earth. "Before you die – confess your sins and ask forgiveness; perhaps, accept the ministration of a priest or minister. Do it just before you die, or you won't make it to heaven." At least, that seems to be the implication.

I would like to urge you to make your peace with God *now* so you can enjoy it for the rest of *this* life, as well as in the life to come. Confess your sin and your need for God's forgiveness, and accept the forgiveness of your sins through Jesus Christ. According to the promise of the Gospel, I say to you: "You are forgiven." Now, go in peace. Be at peace with God.

Once you know that you are forgiven, you can live free of shame, self-condemnation, self-pity and fear. When you know that you're forgiven, you can live in faith, hope, courage, confidence and joy through God's grace. Peace is yours now for the receiving. Peace with God is not just for eternity (though it certainly is that as well); peace with God is for today, for now. And it can be yours.

PRINCIPLE 2: Be at Peace with Yourself

If you know that you are forgiven, you are at peace with God. You can also be at peace with yourself. No more will you condemn yourself or suffer from a burden of guilt and shame over past actions, words, thoughts or neglect. You are forgiven; go and live in peace with yourself. Forgive yourself; God has forgiven you.

Plug into the power source of peace. Many people now have personal computers. If you have one, then you know that a computer has a memory bank which stores up a wealth of information which you program into it. But if you are in the middle of running a program and the plug is pulled out of the power source, you lose everything in the computer memory which was not saved onto a disk. You have to start that file all over again.

That's the way it is in the lives of many people. They are plugged into something that they think will give them peace. But right in the middle of some major problem in their lives, someone pulls the plug. Their "peace" vanishes. It seems that all that is left is a dark, empty screen. Everything that had been accomplished is gone. They have to start all over again.

It is that way in many marriages. The couple is expecting their relationship (or the other person in the relationship) to solve their problems in life. They expect peace and happiness now that they have found the "right person." Everything goes along fine for a while. But just when they think life is under their control, some crisis hits. The other person doesn't "come through" the way they expected. Peace vanishes. Depression sets in. The relationship falls apart. And life hits rock bottom.

Jesus spoke about such a "peace" that depends upon relationships, other people or circumstances. He described it as the peace that the world gives. And He said this: **Peace I leave with you; my peace I give you. I do not give to you as the world gives. Do not let your hearts be troubled and do not be afraid** (John 14:27).

If you want to be at peace with yourself in all circumstances, in every relationship, in the face of every problem, then plug into the power source of continual, lasting peace: Jesus Christ. The peace He gives you will never fade. The screen will never go dark. In the darkest times, Jesus will fill your mind with peace. Don't live in fear; live in hope. Put your full confidence in what Christ is doing through you. Trust in Jesus, not in people or in circumstances; and lasting peace will be yours.

PRINCIPLE 3: Do All You Can to Be at Peace With Others

When you have found peace with God and with yourself, then you are ready to go on to make peace with others. It is possible. You can live peacefully with other people. In many places in the scriptures we are urged to be at peace with others. Here are three:

> **Blessed are the peacemakers, for they will be called sons of God.**
>
> **Matthew 5:9**

> **...seek peace and pursue it.**
> **1 Peter 3:11; Psalm 34:14**

> **If it is possible, as far as it depends on you, live at peace with everyone.**
>
> **Romans 12:18**

Of course, this last verse leaves open the prospect that it may be an impossibility to be at peace with everyone. There are people who will not let you live peacefully with them. They take offense at every word, every gesture, and seemingly every thought. No matter how hard you try to say the right thing or make amends for having said the wrong thing, that other person is hurt, angry, indifferent or hostile toward you.

The key phrase here is: **...as far as it depends on you...** (v. 18). You can't answer for others. You can't live their lives. You can't make them think, feel or act the way you would like. You have to do what you can do, and let them go.

What can you do? What depends on you? The answer to these questions is found in the first three chapters of this section. Have the right attitude toward others – one of compassion, kindness, humility, gentleness and patience. Don't give them a reason to be angry with you. Don't hurt them by your attitude toward them. Don't ignore them, neglect them or ride roughshod over them. Don't tease them. Don't carelessly offend them. Don't badger or provoke or entice them into an argument. Have the right attitude toward others, and you are on your way to being at peace with them.

In the second chapter, we talked about forgiveness. It's hard to say "I'm sorry" when you have done wrong. It's also hard to say "That's all right; I forgive you" when others have done wrong. If we are to live peacefully with others, we must do both: forgive and ask forgiveness. No two people can maintain a relationship for long without one hurting the other. Forgiveness is essential if we are to live in peace.

In the third chapter, we discussed love. If we love others, in the ways described, we will be able to live peacefully with them. You took the checklist test to see how you're doing in this area. If any one of your relationships is unsettled right now, go back and take that test again. Examine your "love life" to see how it's doing. Live peacefully with others – as much as it depends on you.

PRINCIPLE 4: Think Peaceful Thoughts

Peace begins in the mind and heart. So learning to live peacefully begins with how we think. What is in our minds governs how we feel and act. So if we are to change our ways of feeling and acting toward others, we must first change our ways of thinking.

Fill your mind with thoughts of peace, with peaceful thoughts. You can control how you think, you know. Don't let your mind control you. Control your mind and thoughts; bring them into **....obedience to Christ** (2 Cor. 10:5). **...be made new in the attitude of your minds** (Eph. 4:23.) Begin now to take control of your thoughts.

But how do you decide what thoughts are good? What tests do you use to choose the right thoughts over the wrong thoughts? Who will tell you how to think? Listen to these words:

> **...those who live in accordance with the Spirit have their minds set on what the Spirit desires...the mind controlled by the Spirit is life and peace.**
> **Romans 8:5,6**

The Spirit of God – God Himself – is the One to tell us how to think. He tells us in several ways. Through the scriptures, we have in written form much of what He wants us to know about how to think and act. Through the teaching and preaching of those who have studied the scriptures and dedicated their lives to God, we can receive good, sound guidance in thinking and acting. Then the Spirit works in our minds, hearts and lives to convict and convince us of the truth and of right thinking. Listen to that voice within; it may be God speaking to you. Let your mind be controlled by the Spirit.

> **Finally, brothers, whatever is true ... noble ... right ... pure ... lovely ... admirable — if anything is excellent or praiseworthy — think about such things.**
>
> **Philippians 4:8**

Add to this list the things with which you know God wants you to fill your mind. Then begin to do them. Fill your mind with those things. Control your thoughts by thinking about those things.

Some of the things I would add to this list include thoughts which are: quiet, peaceful, beautiful, creative, inspiring, gentle, humble, compassionate. Any of us could go on from there. I hope you will. Make your own list, and use it.

One thing we need to do in our hectic lifestyle is to stop now and then and enjoy a bit of solitude. It is difficult to think peaceful thoughts when we are caught up in the noise and confusion of work or school or family life. When others are talking, cars are honking, machines are whirring, radios are blasting, telephones are ringing, children are crying, adults are complaining, and on and on – it is hard to maintain a calm, peaceful spirit.

The way to begin making a change in your unsettled lifestyle is to set aside a certain amount of time each day –

preferably at the same time – when you can be away from any noise or distraction. Spend the time studying scripture, praying, reading inspirational books, or singing spiritual songs, praising and worshiping the Lord – whatever is comfortable for you, whatever benefits your peace of mind. But along with all of these things, or perhaps in place of some of them, spend some time in quiet, uninterrupted meditation. As you meditate, try not to think of anything. Make an effort to clear your mind of everything for a few minutes. Relax. Breathe deeply. Concentrate. Shut out the world, everything except God. Listen for the divine voice. Listen. Don't talk. Be silent.

As you begin to discover the peaceful thoughts that will come into your mind during these times, hold on to them. Let them fill your mind at other times as well. Let these times of peaceful thinking begin to control your thoughts in the midst of noise and confusion and continual distractions. Learn to concentrate at other times on peaceful thoughts. Learn the secret of solitude in the midst of a multitude.

PRINCIPLE 5: *Renew Your Peace in Prayer*

No one is always at peace. All of us are, at times, troubled and distracted by the circumstances of our lives. I am not always at peace within myself or with others. Are you? What, then, should we do when our peace grows weak? How do we renew our peace?

The Apostle Paul tells us:

> **Do not be anxious about anything, but in everything, by prayer and petition, with thanksgiving, present your requests to God. And the peace of**

**God, which transcends all understanding, will
guard your hearts and your minds in Christ Jesus.**
Philippians 4:6,7

We renew our peace through prayer. We find where
the plug has been pulled and plug it in again. We go back
to the One Who promised to give us continual, lasting
peace, and we talk to Him about what has robbed us of
our peace. Prayer is talking to God about our problems
and needs, about what's happening in our lives; and, perhaps, it's asking Him to do something about it or to show
us what to do. Prayer and petition, with thanksgiving –
this is the key to renewing your peace of mind.

Refuse to be at odds with yourself. Refuse to be at
odds with others. Make up your mind to be at peace with
yourself and others; and when you realize you've lost that
peacefulness, pray. Pray – and be at peace.

Exercises for the Self-Esteem Builder

1. Make a list (long or short) of everything for which you feel guilty or ashamed. Then go down the list one item at a time and say: "Lord, I'm sorry. Thank You for forgiving me through Jesus Christ." Then cross that item off the list. Believe that you are forgiven. And be at peace with God.

2. Write down the names of three persons with whom you find it hard to live in peace. Next to each name, write down anything *you* can possibly do to make peace with that person. Go and do it. Review your list each day for two weeks to see how you are doing.

3. Use the list of things to think about (from Phil. 4:8) to start a list of at least 25 things that you can concentrate on when you want to think peaceful thoughts. Keep the list with you; and, for the next two weeks, whenever your thoughts threaten your peace of mind, choose something from that list to think about.

4. For one month, try the suggestions for a time of peace and meditation. Use your imagination. Find something comfortable for you, but stick with it every day for a month.

5. Keep a prayer journal for three months. In the front of it, write down the names of five persons in whom you want to build self-esteem. Don't let a day pass without praying for each one. Record your own experiences each day as you renew your own peace through prayer, and as you see prayer helping you and them to live peacefully with each other.

5

Be Thankful for Others

It may seem like a trite statement, but Thanksgiving *should* come more than once a year. Every day should be set aside for the giving of thanks – for others. Thankfulness is an attitude, one that should be translated into action. If we are to be thankful for others, we should give thanks for them. We should make a daily habit of giving thanks to God for those around us.

In 1 Timothy 4:4,5 we read:

...everything God created is good, and nothing is to be rejected if it is received with thanksgiving, because it is consecrated by the word of God and prayer.

Christians have traditionally used that passage as a basis for giving thanks at meals. But it certainly goes far beyond habitual prayers at mealtimes.

If we change this passage only slightly, it could read this way:

Everyone God created is good, and no one is to be rejected if he/she is received with thanksgiving, because he/she is consecrated by the word of God and prayer.

If everything God created is good, then people are good. We human beings are the best of God's creation. For all of our sin and weakness, we are still created to be good; and we should receive each other with thanksgiving.

PRINCIPLE 5: Be Thankful for Others

We could summarize this passage this way: *Don't reject – do receive.* Don't reject others; do receive them as persons worthy of respect and love. Treat them with the honor due to everything God has created.

Here are some *do's and don'ts* to serve as a guide to proper treatment of others:

Don't Cuss

When we get a little angry and say things we shouldn't about others, we are verbally rejecting them. Critical and hateful words directed toward others are one form of rejection. Don't do it; don't reject other people because of their attitude or actions. Don't reject others because of their personality or how they dress or how they talk or who their friends are. Don't reject others for any reason. And don't cuss them – don't say hateful and critical things about them.

Maybe your son did get a "D" in math (and it was your favorite subject in school). But don't be critical of him because of his failure. Don't cuss him. Help him. Tutor him. Spend time with him as he works to improve his grade. Encourage him. He can do better next time.

Pick someone in your life: your spouse, a child, a friend, anyone. (Keep this person in mind as we think through the rest of this chapter. Let's say it's a "him.") What does that person do or say (or neglect to do or say) that makes you so upset? How do you respond to him? Don't cuss him. Don't be critical, hateful, resentful or spiteful. Don't tear down his self-esteem. Build it up.

Don't Fuss

Don't nag. Don't pick at all the little things the other person does wrong. Don't be always trying to change him. Instead, work at changing yourself.

"But he's the one with the problem!" you may say.

Sure, he has a problem, more than one. He's not perfect. He does have some changing to do. But if you are "cussing" and fussing at him, instead of being thankful for him, then you need to change. If you're rejecting him by being critical and hateful, you need to improve *your* attitude.

Now we are back to the double benefit of self-esteem building. If you adopt an attitude of thankfulness toward this person, you will feel better about yourself *and him*.

Don't Muss

Yes, *muss* really is a word. It means "to put into disorder, to create confusion" – which is precisely what an attitude of rejecting others does. Are you continually misunderstanding what the other person says? Then listen more closely. Does he accuse you of constantly ignoring him? He may be right. Take a good look at your attitude. Constantly misunderstanding and ignoring the other person is one way of rejecting him. Don't muss up your relationship. Turn it around.

Begin to be thankful for that other person, the one who causes you so much pain and sorrow. Give thanks to God that he is alive. Thank God for your relationship with him, whatever it is and whatever it has been like. Let God "consecrate" it. Let Him renew it. Let God change your attitude and your relationship.

Don't reject. Do give thanks.

Do Assume Good Things

As your attitude begins to change, your relationship will start to change, too. Accept the other person as he is, with all his faults and weaknesses and "stupid" ways (as you see them). Accept him as he is, where he is. Then begin to expect better of him – not as a negative attitude of "I wish he would change," but as a positive attitude of "I know he can do better." Expect better, and he will give it.

But don't expect better of the other person and then simply sit back and watch to see what happens. Work with him to improve, to change what he wants to change. Work with him constantly, consistently, to bring out the very best that's in him. Let him know that you expect the best from him, and in time he will come to expect it of himself.

Do Assure Him of Your Trust

Your relationship with this other person will be strengthened by your assuring him of your trust. When you ask him to do something, give him a chance to do it. Give him time; give him "space." Let him know that you believe in him, that you trust him to do what you have asked of him.

"What if he fails? He has failed before, hasn't he? Maybe he will do so again."

So what? Have you never failed? Have you always succeeded at everything you've attempted, in every part of your relationship with him? If he fails, help him to try again. Assure him of your continual trust. Continue to expect the best of him, and continue to work with him to bring out his full potential.

And be patient. There is a a popular saying going around: "Be patient with me; God isn't finished with me yet." What we want *from* others, we must be willing to give *to* others. If you want the other person to be patient with you, then be patient with him – God isn't finished with him yet either.

Believe in him. Don't always be questioning everthing he does. Don't ask him to explain everything he says: "Just what did you mean by that remark?" Give him the benefit of the doubt. Give him a chance to prove himself, to show you that your trust in him is well-placed.

Do Assist Him with What You Expect from Him

Tell him clearly what you expect. Don't make him guess. Don't tell him just enough to make him think he understands, only to find out he doesn't. Don't assume he understands whatever you say to him. Spell out as clearly as possible what you want from him so there is no misunderstanding about what you expect.

Do all you can to help the other person live up to your highest expectations of him. Help willingly and patiently. Don't be a martyr: "I don't see why he can't get this done without *my* help." Maybe he just likes your company. Perhaps he could do it alone, but he likes to work with you. Maybe he really does need your help. Why deny him that help if it's what he needs to do his very best? You should feel honored to be needed.

Conclusion

This list of *do's and don'ts* is not exhaustive, but it's a good beginning. You can add your own suggestions to the list. But remember the main point here: if you want to build up self-esteem in another person, don't reject him; rather, accept him with thanksgiving. To build self-esteem in someone else, live in a way that will give that person confidence that you have accepted him and do love him.

Exercises for the Self-Esteem Builder

1. Carry a pocket notebook with you for a week. Write down in it every phrase you use that is critical or hateful, that tears down self-esteem instead of building it. At the end of the week, make a commitment not to use these negative phrases again. Then burn the notebook as a sign of your commitment.

2. Choose one person with whom you have a close relationship. Make a list of things you could change about yourself that would make the relationship better. Concentrate on making those changes. Carry the list with you for one month to check your progress.

3. Talk with the other person about trust. Have him join you in writing down your answers to this question: "How do I feel about _____ when he/she doesn't trust me?" Then spend at least 10 minutes discussing your answers with each other. Repeat this exercise once a week for three weeks.

4. Finish this sentence in at least 10 ways:

   I can help _____ *do better by....*

5. Add at least three more *do's and don'ts* to the list in this chapter.

6

Learn from Each Other

**Let the word of Christ dwell in you richly as
you teach and admonish one another with all wisdom....**

Colossians 3:16

A good teacher first has to be a good learner.
Teaching requires learning. If there is no one to learn, there
is no need for a teacher.

So the implication of this verse is that before we can
become teachers we must first become disciples (in the
true sense of that word). Before we start trying to teach
one another, we should have it as our goal to learn from
one another. If we are going to become self-esteem
builders, we must adopt the attitude of learners.

PRINCIPLE 6: Learn from Each Other

Let me suggest these ABC's of Learning:

Acknowledge the other person's insight.

Build on a good foundation.

Challenge the other person.

Acknowledge the Other Person's Insight

One of the hardest things for any of us to accept is
the fact that someone else may know more than we do.
The ability to recognize the limits of one's own knowledge
is called humility. And it's tough for us to develop.

Oh, if we are questioned directly about our knowledge of any subject, we will naturally say, "Of course, I don't know everything about it yet." But when we get into a disagreement or dispute about anything, most of us tend to act as if we *do* know everything about it. It really doesn't matter what the subject is. Our pride won't allow us to let the other person think we don't know what we are talking about. That kind of "know-it-all" attitude keeps us from learning anything new.

No matter how educated or enlightened we may think we are, we need the humility to admit that the other person may have insight that we don't have. We can easily admit that we don't know *everything*. But to admit that the other person may know *more than we do* about anything "goes against the grain" for most of us. Yet learning demands a humble attitude, one that can say to another, "You really seem to know more about this than I do; I'll listen and learn."

If we are going to be learners, we can't always be teachers. In fact, the best teachers are aware that they are always learning, that they have not yet fully arrived. So be both a good teacher *and* a good disciple by adopting the attitude of a learner in your relationship with other people.

This kind of humility is especially hard for parents to exhibit in their relationship with their children. Parents fall naturally into the role of teachers. They are older, more experienced and, supposedly, wiser. They have a great deal to teach their children about life, maturity and responsibility. But sometimes children, in their moments of special insight, can help parents see things more clearly, if the parents will only listen and learn.

It's hard for children too, especially adolescents, to see themselves as learners. By the time most youngsters get into their teens, they are often convinced that they know more about life than their parents do. They think they can stop learning.

In the same way, it's hard for pastors to learn from those who are not theologically trained. It's hard for employers to learn from employees, supervisors to learn from new line workers, older adults to learn from younger adults. It's not easy to be a learner, but for the self-esteem builder, it is essential.

The two-part rule of learning is: *listen and learn.* Stop trying so hard to figure it all out for yourself. Listen to the instructions. Listen to others who have been through the same experience you are going through. Listen to those who have insight into your problem, even if they haven't experienced it themselves personally. Listen to them. Once you have listened, then learn from what you have heard. Put it into practice. Go and do it. Follow through with the advice you've received.

Listen. And learn.

Build on a Good Foundation

Along the coast in Southern California, houses are sometimes washed into the sea because they aren't built on a good, solid foundation. In the same way, many people are awash in a torrent of troubles because their lives have not been built on a firm foundation. Our text (Col. 3:16) tells us what kind of foundation we need for our lives. If we are going to teach and learn from each other, we need to do so on the foundation of the Word of Christ.

In Matthew 7:24-27, Jesus tells of a wise man who built his house on the rock, and it withstood the wind, rain and flood. Then He tells of a foolish man who built his house on the sand, and it was washed away in the flood waters. He summarizes His lesson in these words: **Therefore everyone who hears these words of mine and puts them into practice is like a wise man who built his house on the rock** (v. 24). The foundation for Christian learning is the accumulated wisdom of the teachings of Christ. (And beyond those teachings, the words of the New Testament and the rest of scripture, which the Church has traditionally called "the Word of God.")

Much of what is written today about building self-esteem falls far short of the mark because it is not built on the foundation of the Word of Christ. Much of it is true. Much of it is good. But it doesn't go far enough for the child of God. Any Christian idea of self-esteem must be founded on the Gospel of Christ and the teachings of Jesus.

Our self-esteem comes from who we are in Christ.

If we are going to learn from each other in ways that will build up our self-esteem, we must be learning the truth according to the Word of Christ.

Begin with the Gospels, with the words and teachings of Christ. He tells us what God thinks of us: **You are the salt of the earth ... the light of the world** (Matt. 5:13,14). He tells us that, as the children of God, we have the power and authority to change the world. In fact, I think He tells us that we have the responsibility to change the world – to more fully bring in the Kingdom of God. We are important: the world needs us.

Teach and learn from the rest of the New Testament, which is our primary source of knowledge and instruction in how to live and think. If we believe in Jesus Christ, we are the children of God. Our heavenly Father has promised us fantastic gifts and powers. He expects us to use these gifts and powers to the fullest extent in this world. The New Testament tells us of God's love, grace, mercy and transforming power in which we all can share. What better way to build up our self-esteem?

Go on to the Old Testament, which is the foundation for the knowledge of the New Testament and which should be included in a full program of spiritual and practical instruction. It tells us about the beginnings of God's work in the world and of the history of the people of God. It tells us more about the future of our world and of the Kingdom of God. It provides important background for us in understanding the New Testament. It helps us, too, to see how important God's people are to the rest of the world.

Remember, though, that the important thing is not what you learn, but how you put into practice what you have learned. Learning names, places and doctrines, memorizing Bible verses and being able to explain prophecies – all of these things are only preliminary. The real learning takes place when we understand better how to live, when we know more about who we are, and when we begin to live as God intended for us to live.

Challenge the Other Person

What we are doing is learning from each other. It has to be mutual. We teach each other; and we learn from each other. An important part of that mutual learning process is challenging other persons to live according to what they have taught us.

Put into practice what you have learned from the other person. Provide the example of living which you have learned; and thereby challenge the other person to live up to what he has taught you.

Discover new insights into the scriptures as you continue to study them yourself in more depth. Then share your insights with your teacher/learner/friend.

Be accountable to each other. Don't let the other person off too easy by excusing attitudes and behavior which are contrary to what he has been teaching you. Follow through yourself by living up to what you have learned; hold your teacher accountable, too. And, of course, be accountable to your friend for what you are teaching and learning. Put into practice together the things you are learning together.

Conclusion

Adopt the attitude of a learner. It's a good way to build self-esteem in the other person. Let him be your teacher. Learn from him. But teach him, too. And, together, live up to what you are learning. Grow together in your self-esteem as you grow together in your knowledge, understanding and practice of the Word of Christ.

Exercises for the Self-Esteem Builder

1. Write the names of five persons with whom you have a good relationship. Next to each name write at least one thing you could learn from that person because you know he or she has insight into that area.

Choose one person to do these things with:

2. Read through the Gospels and mark the words of Christ, stopping to meditate on those which apply to your life.

3. Read the New Testament, from Romans through Jude, to mark those portions that talk about how we should live our lives. Spend extra time thinking through the parts that apply most directly to you.

4. As you study the Bible, keep a journal in which you write down everything you read about how important you are; write down *why* you are important.

5. Devise a system of accountability between you and the other person. Make a commitment to each other to follow through with that system for a period of at least six months.

7

Worship the Lord Together

Don't be put off by the spiritual-sounding title of this last chapter, our seventh step toward becoming self-esteem builders. This final principle is just as practical as every other step and has to be taken along with all the others. No step can be taken in isolation; they interact with one another.

PRINCIPLE 7: Worship the Lord Together

> ...sing psalms, hymns and spiritual songs with gratitude in your hearts to God. And whatever you do, whether in word or deed, do it all in the name of the Lord Jesus, giving thanks to God the Father through him.
>
> Colossians 3:16,17

> Do you not know that your body is a temple of the Holy Spirit, who is in you, whom you have received from God? You are not your own; you were bought at a price. Therefore honor God with your body.
>
> 1 Corinthians 6:19,20

On the basis of these two texts, I would like to suggest two potentially life-transforming principles:

PRINCIPLE 1: We Worship the Lord by Honoring Him in All We Do – in Body, Mind and Spirit

We could say that we should be "wholly holy" – totally dedicated to honoring God in body, mind and spir-

273

it. To be holy is to be set apart for a specific purpose; namely, to honor God. We should recognize holiness as the proper attitude of our lives, and therefore set ourselves apart from anything in this world that would not honor our heavenly Father. In fact, any attitude or action that would dishonor God should be considered inappropriate for us. Desire for personal holiness should then be the motivating force for all that we do with our bodies, all that we allow in our minds, and all that we yield to in our spirits.

This attitude of total dedication is called, in Romans 12:1,2, our "spiritual worship":

> **Therefore, I urge you, brothers, in view of God's mercy, to offer your bodies as living sacrifices, holy and pleasing to God – which is your spiritual worship. Do not conform any longer to the pattern of this world, but be transformed by the renewing of your mind. Then you will be able to test and approve what God's will is – his good, pleasing and perfect will.**

What would give greater glory to God than to do His perfect will? What is better and more honorable than to be holy and pleasing to God? The best form of worship is to be totally dedicated to God in all we do – in body, mind and spirit.

PRINCIPLE 2: We Honor God by Honoring What He Has Created

The context of 1 Corinthians 6:19,20 has to do with keeping ourselves from sexual immorality, and thus honoring God in our bodies. I would suggest that when we keep ourselves from sexual immorality, we honor the other person by respecting the sanctity of both persons in body, mind and spirit. The total person is involved in sexual intercourse. There can be no divorce of the body from the mind or the spirit in such an intimate state.

God created all human beings, and He intends for us to honor ourselves, and all other humans, with our whole being. To honor God is to use what He has given us, within the limits He has set for us, for the purpose for which we were created. God created us, for instance, with the intention that one man and one woman would be united for life in a relationship that would provide lifelong intimacy and companionship. This union of man and woman was meant to be one that would normally result in children and family relationships which would continue through generations to come. Any relationship that is opposed to that purpose, or that threatens that intended state, dishonors both creature and Creator.

By extension of this thought, then, I believe that *whatever we do that honors other people also honors their Creator, and is thereby a means of worshiping God.* If we dishonor other persons, whom God has created, we are committing blasphemy.[1] And, by the same token, if we honor other persons, we are worshiping God. We honor others by respecting their sanctity. They were created, as we all were, to be holy – to be dedicated to the glory of God, to be set apart to honor God in body, mind and spirit. When we deny that right to other human beings, we are dishonoring God. When we extend that created right to all

---

[1] *Blasphemy* is defined by *The Random House Dictionary of the English Language* as "an impious utterance or action concerning God or sacred things." So I think it is an appropriate term for the dishonoring of other people who were created in the image and likeness of God.

human beings, we are honoring and worshiping God together.

How do we deny that right to others? In what ways? Here are a few possibilities:

If we engage in sexual union with someone other than our spouse, as we have already mentioned, we dishonor that person, our mate and our God.

If, because of their race or color or religion or nationality, we deny, even by our attitude, other people's right to be fully human, we dishonor what God has created and thereby dishonor the Creator.

If we deny freedom – when it is in our power to grant it – to other human beings because of race, nationality, religion, etc., we dishonor them and God.

If we have the resources to help people conquer their poverty, but withhold that assistance from them, we dishonor those people and their divine Creator.

If we destroy life, or threaten its destruction, by releasing toxic wastes into our environment without proper safeguards for the health and safety of others, we dishonor our heavenly Father and the human lives He has created.

If we continue to build nuclear arms, and other weapons of destruction – far beyond any necessary limits – and thereby threaten all living things, we dishonor God and His creation.

If we abuse the body, mind and spirit of another human being (a child, a spouse or anyone else), we dishonor both that person and the Creator.

To honor God is to worship Him. And to honor human beings is to honor God.

Therefore, our worship of God includes the many ways our lives affect the lives of others. If we, by our attitudes and actions, work to build up self-esteem in others, thus causing them to honor God more, we are thereby worshiping God. *So we need to worship the Lord together by a mutual building-up of self-esteem.*

Transformational Action (T.A.)

A few years ago, Dr. Thomas Harris wrote a book called, *I'm OK, You're OK,* in which he introduced what he called Transactional Analysis (or T.A.). Let me suggest here a new kind of T.A. which will help us put into practice these two principles of honoring God.

I call this concept *Transformational Action.* The idea for it goes back to our text from Romans 12:

> **Do not conform any longer to the pattern of this world, but *be transformed* by the renewing of your mind. Then you will be able to test and approve what God's will is – his good, pleasing and perfect will.** (emphasis mine)
>
> **Romans 12:2**

We need to be transformed in our minds so we will be transformed in our actions. A total change, from one way of living to another, is what is needed. We need to refuse any longer to live according to the attitudes that surround us: lust, racial hatred, greed, hunger for political power, violence, nationalistic fervor.[2] We must reject all these attitudes as dishonoring to God. We must begin to allow God to transform us within, knowing that as He does so, our lives will be transformed as well. When we have undergone this total transformation, we will begin to do those things, even in our bodies, that will honor Him. And the things that honor God will be the things that honor other human beings.

Transformational action is doing those things which honor God by honoring His creation.

God created our bodies. Therefore, we need to refuse to put into or on our bodies anything that does not benefit or beautify them. God created our minds. Therefore, we must determine to put into our minds only those things that will benefit them. God created us to be holy temples for Himself – places of residence for His Spirit. Therefore, we must treat our bodies and minds with the same reverence we would show any holy temple. In fact, we should treat the temple of our bodies with *more* reverence, because God does not dwell in temples made by human hands,[3] but in those places of His choosing: our bodies.

Transformational action is doing those things toward other human beings that honor God by honoring them. God created them, too – their bodies, minds and

---

[2] Nationalistic fervor is not the same as patriotism. It is an attitude that leads to exploitation and domination of other countries.

[3] See Acts 17:24.

spirits. Any attitude, action or word which benefits or beautifies or builds up the other person honors God. And any attitude, action or word that harms, desecrates or tears down another person dishonors God. One is worship; the other is blasphemy.

Think of every person on earth as a special creation of God, and treat each one with the respect due to God's highest creation. Think of every human being as a potential temple of God, and treat each one with the reverence due His temple. Think of each person as one who was created for the glory and honor of the Creator, and do all in your power to make it possible for each one to live in that way.

This attitude provides a sound basis for all that we do in the Church:

- Christian evangelism, bringing people to God through Christ;
- Relief work, helping millions in their poverty;
- Counseling, helping individuals to be healthy in mind and spirit;
- Political action, responding to the needs of desperate people in society;
- Global peacemaking efforts, paving the way for lasting peace; and
- Programs to curb abuse, whether it be drugs, sex or violence.

With this mutual attitude, we will work together toward solving problems of unemployment, crime, pornography, injustice, hunger, poverty and the threats to international peace. And in working together in this way, we will be worshiping the Lord together.

As Christians, as God's own dear children, may our faith-affirmation be:

Whatever we do, whether in word or action, we will do it all in the name of the Lord Jesus.

Exercises for the Self-Esteem Builder

1. Make a list of what you consider to be the 10 greatest problems that people face in today's world. For each one, answer this question: "How does the problem keep people from honoring God in their lives?"

    For each of these 10 problems, answer the question: "How can the Church respond in order to solve this problem?"

2. Write a few paragraphs, in your own words, in which you answer the following questions:

    a. "How does honoring other human beings also honor God?"

    b. "Where do I need to be changed – transformed – in my attitudes and actions?"

3. Choose one problem in which you have some expertise and interest in helping to solve during the next few years. Set some goals for yourself in this effort. Answer this question: "How do you think the problem can be solved, and where do you intend to begin?"

Part V:
The Last Word

Catch the Vision

This book is not meant to be the last word on this subject. No one should have the last word on a subject as vital as this one. We need to be continually exploring the issue, discussing the many sides to it, and discovering more effective ways to communicate to the world what we are talking about.

The issue of self-esteem is certainly not the new gospel for a new day; but it is intricately woven into the Gospel of Jesus Christ. And we are not suggesting replacing the making of disciples with the preparing of leaders; rather, we are saying that these two aspects of the Christian mission are one and the same thing.

A disciple of Jesus Christ should be a leader in the secular realm. Our Lord sent us out to literally change the world; and in order to accomplish that task, we need leaders: persons who are mature, responsible and able to take the initiative in decision-making among their peers. The preparing of people in our churches to be the leaders of tomorrow demands that we build self-esteem in them as a necessary foundation for leadership.

Many of us share a vision of churches around the world which are building self-esteem in their people through preaching, teaching and the fostering of healthy relationships. We have a vision of Christians going out from our churches into the world – into their jobs, homes and businesses, into schools, theaters, legislatures and community groups – and becoming leaders wherever they go. We envision such people taking the lead in making the decisions that will benefit the greatest number of people in our world.

Catch the vision. Share that vision with us.

Hear the Challenge

If you are willing to share that vision, then please *hear the challenge.*

The challenge our churches face is the initiation of a new reformation. We need to reform our preaching and teaching, our theology, our liturgical practices, and, most of all, our relationships. We need to be transformed through the power of Jesus Christ into the Church which He envisioned – a people scattered around the world bringing light into the darkness, bringing the estranged children of God back to their Father in heaven.

But to accomplish this objective, we need to make some major changes in our theology and practices. We need to think, preach and act as if every human being is important. The Church, as a whole, has not been doing these things. We need to believe that people's lives here on earth are important, rather than claiming that all that really matters is their eternal destiny. If we are not interested in people's famine, freedom and family life, we are not truly interested in their salvation.

We must reform our thinking so that we see every human being as a special act of God's creation, as a part of God's new creation through Jesus Christ, and therefore as a person of vital importance. Such an attitude will work to break down racial hatred, nationalistic frenzy, violence, sexual abuse, religious bigotry, and all other sins of humanity. The Church must take the lead in accomplishing this task in the next century by preparing people who understand the value of each human being.

Develop an Understanding

If you have caught the vision and heard the challenge, you are ready to *develop an understanding*.

The issues of self-esteem and leadership cannot be fully understood apart from Christian theology. We need more than a psychological or sociological view of these issues; such views only take us part way to our goal. If we have read everything that has been written on these issues in other fields (education, business, psychology, sociology, etc.), we have only just begun to understand the situation.

Self-esteem is the inner confidence that is generated within us by knowing who we are in Christ as the children of God, forgiven and freed from our fears. Leadership is best exercised by those who have spiritual maturity, those who are accountable to God, so that our natural desires (which have been corrupted by sin) will be controlled and corrected by the inner power of God.

As we develop a better understanding of these issues from a theological perspective, we need to change our view of theology. I have offered a definition of theology as a systematic understanding of the relationship between God and human beings. The Church has always built its system of theology around Who God is and what our human responsibility is toward Him. I have suggested here that we build a system of thought around who we are and what God has intended for us to be.

Why should we change our theology from a God-centered approach to a human-centered one? Because we are failing to communicate with our world. We are failing to reach people with the Gospel of Jesus Christ. They aren't hearing what we're saying because they think we're not saying anything that relates to their situation in life. But if we begin where they are, and speak to the needs which they know they have, if we tell them who they can become in Christ, and then lead them by our example into a new and better way of living, I believe they will listen. At least more of them will.

We are not for a moment taking our eyes off the central mission of the Church, which is to make disciples of all nations. On the contrary, fulfillment of that mission is exactly what I am proposing. I am convinced that we can be more effective in making disciples of all nations if we will reform our theology from a God-centered approach to a human-centered one, in order to provide a positive basis for preaching to people "where they live."

Whatever their situation in life, people need, most of all, the hope and confidence generated by the Gospel-promise that they can become all that God intended them to be. They need self-esteem. Those who are brought to Christ through this approach will be better prepared to provide sound leadership for our world in coming generations.

Make It Work

If you have caught the vision, heard the challenge and begun to develop a better understanding of this approach, then you are ready to *make it work*. You are ready to go about the work of building self-esteem in others, which is an important part of making disciples.

Those who are fearful, self-condemning, depressed and lonely, those who are resentful, angry and abusive – such people are not living up to their potential as God intended. As the Church of Jesus Christ, part of our job – a major portion of our work – is to help people discover a new life in Christ and to live it out in their daily existence. Only in that way can we prepare them to be leaders. Only in that way will the Gospel that we preach make any sense to the world.

If people are not believers in Christ, they can be brought to Him most effectively by those who live the kind of life described in the fourth section of this book. If they are believers, but are living in fear, guilt and anger, they need others who will help them build up their self-esteem, for that is what they lack. Many people have faith (or think they do), yet are almost totally lacking in self-esteem. This situation keeps them locked into a lifestyle that is not at all Christ-like.

If we Christians are to provide the sound leadership which our world so desperately needs, we must have a healthy self-esteem and the confidence, hope and faith generated by knowing who we are in Christ.

Conclusion

So I don't have the last word. I only have these final words of challenge and encouragement: *build up self-esteem in others, preparing both yourself and them for leadership in tomorrow's world.*

Bibliography

Blanchard, Kenneth and Johnson, Spencer. *The One Minute Manager*. New York: Berkley Books, 1981.

Burns, James MacGregor. *Leadership*. New York: Harper & Row, Publishers, 1978.

Geneen, Harold with Moscow, Alvin. *Managing*. Garden City: Doubleday & Company, Inc., 1984.

Girard, Joe with Brown, Stanley H. *How to Sell Anything to Anybody*. New York: Warner Books, 1977.

Harris, Thomas A. *I'm OK – You're OK: A Practical Guide to Transactional Analysis*. New York: Harper & Row, Publishers, 1967.

The Holy Bible: New International Version. Grand Rapids: Zondervan Bible Publishers, 1978.

Iacocca, Lee with Novak, William. *Iacocca: An Autobiography*. New York: Bantam Books, 1984.

The Living Bible, Paraphrased. Wheaton: Tyndale House, Publishers, 1971.

Maccoby, Michael. *The Leader: A New Face for American Management*. New York: Ballantine Books, 1981.

McCarthy, John J. *Why managers fail...and what to do about it*. New York: McGraw-Hill Publications Company, 1978.

McConkey, Dale D. *How to Manage by Results*, 4th Ed. American Management Association, 1983.

McCormack, Mark H. *What They Don't Teach You at Harvard Business School.* New York: Bantam Books, 1984.

Naisbitt, John. *Megatrends: Ten New Directions Transforming Our Lives.* New York: Warner Books, 1982.

Peters, Thomas J. and Waterman, Robert H., Jr. *In Search of Excellence: Lessons from America's Best-Run Companies.* New York: Warner Books, 1982.

And these books from Robert H. Schuller:

Discover Your Possibilities. Eugene: Harvest House Publishers, 1978.

It's Possible. Old Tappan: Fleming H. Revell Company, 1978.

Reach Out for New Life. New York: Hawthorn Books, Inc., Publishers, 1977.

Self-Esteem: The New Reformation. Waco: Word Books, 1982.

Self-Love: The Dynamic Force for Success. Old Tappan: Fleming H. Revell Company, 1969.

The Be-Happy Attitudes. Waco: Word Books, 1985.

Tough-Minded Faith for Tender-Hearted People. New York: Bantam Books, 1983.

Tough Times Never Last, but Tough People Do! Nashville: Thomas Nelson Publishers, 1983.

You Can Become the Person You Want to Be. New York: Pillar Books, 1973.

To contact Jimmy Reader write: 412 S. F • Wellington, KS • 67152

Additional copies of this book are available from your local bookstore or by writing:

Harrison House: P. O. Box 35035 • Tulsa, OK • 74153